THE
COLLECTED WORKS
of
W. H. HUDSON

———

IN TWENTY-FOUR
VOLUMES

A LITTLE BOY LOST
AND VARIOUS POEMS

A
LITTLE BOY LOST

TOGETHER WITH THE POEMS OF

W. H. HUDSON

AMS PRESS
NEW YORK

Reprinted with the permission of J. M. Dent and Sons, Ltd.
From the edition of 1923, London
First AMS EDITION published 1968
Manufactured in the United States of America

Library of Congress Catalogue Card Number: 68-58908

AMS PRESS, INC.
New York, N.Y. 10003

NOTE

It has been thought desirable that the small content of W. H. Hudson's verse writings be assembled in one book, and to the story of *A Little Boy Lost* in this volume the Publishers have appended all such authentic poems as can be found. Of these the most important, the ballad of *The Old Man of Kensington Gardens,* is here made public for the first time.

CONTENTS

A LITTLE BOY LOST

POEMS

A LITTLE BOY LOST

A LITTLE BOY LOST

CHAPTER I

THE HOME ON THE GREAT PLAIN

SOME like to be one thing, some another. There is so much to be done, so many different things to do, so many trades! Shepherds, soldiers, sailors, ploughmen, carters—one could go on all day naming without getting to the end of them. For myself, boy and man, I have been many things, working for a living, and sometimes doing things just for pleasure; but somehow, whatever I did, it never seemed quite the right and proper thing to do—it never quite satisfied me. I always wanted to do something else—I wanted to be a carpenter. It seemed to me that to stand among wood-shavings and sawdust, making things at a bench with bright, beautiful tools out of nice-smelling wood, was the cleanest, healthiest, prettiest work that any man can do. Now all this has nothing, or very little, to do with my story; I only spoke of it because I had to begin somehow, and it struck me that I would make a start that way. And for another reason, too. *His father was a carpenter.* I mean Martin's father— Martin, the Little Boy Lost. His father's name was John, and he was a very good man and a good carpenter, and he loved to do his carpentering better

than anything else; in fact, as much as I should have
loved it if I had been taught that trade. He lived
in a seaside town, named Southampton, where there
is a great harbour, where he saw great ships coming
and going to and from all parts of the world. Now,
no strong, brave man can live in a place like that,
seeing the ships and often talking to the people
who voyaged in them about the distant lands where
they had been, without wishing to go and see those
distant countries for himself. When it is winter in
England, and it rains and rains, and the east wind
blows, and it is grey and cold, and the trees are bare,
who does not think how nice it would be to fly away
like the summer birds to some distant country where
the sky is always blue and the sun shines bright and
warm every day? And so it came to pass that John,
at last, when he was an old man, sold his shop, and
went abroad. They went to a country many thousands of miles away—for you must know that Mrs.
John went too; and when the sea voyage ended,
they travelled many days and weeks in a waggon
until they came to the place where they wanted to
live; and there, in that lonely country, they built
a house, and made a garden, and planted an orchard.
It was a desert, and they had no neighbours, but they
were happy enough because they had as much land
as they wanted, and the weather was always bright
and beautiful; John, too, had his carpenter's tools to
work with when he felt inclined; and, best of all,
they had little Martin to love and think about.

But how about Martin himself? You might think

that with no other child to prattle to and play with or even to see, it was too lonely a home for him. Not a bit of it! No child could have been happier. He did not want for company; his playfellows were the dogs and cats and chickens, and any creature in and about the house. But most of all he loved the little shy creatures that lived in the sunshine among the flowers—the small birds and butterflies, and little beasties and creeping things he was accustomed to see outside the gate among the tall, wild sunflowers. There were acres of these plants, and they were taller than Martin, and covered with flowers no bigger than marigolds, and here among the sunflowers he used to spend most of the day, as happy as possible.

He had other amusements, too. Whenever John went to his carpenter's shop—for the old man still dearly loved his carpentering—Martin would run in to keep him company. One thing he liked to do was to pick up the longest wood-shavings, to wind them round his neck and arms and legs, and then he would laugh and dance with delight, happy as a young Indian in his ornaments.

A wood-shaving may seem a poor plaything to a child with all the toyshops in London to pick and choose from, but it is really very curious and pretty. Bright and smooth to the touch, pencilled with delicate wavy lines, while in its spiral shape it reminds one of winding plants and tendrils by means of which vines and creepers support themselves, and flowers with curling petals, and curled leaves and sea-shells and many other pretty natural objects.

One day Martin ran into the house looking very flushed and joyous, holding up his pinafore with something heavy in it.

"What have you got now?" cried his father and mother in a breath, getting up to peep at his treasure, for Martin was always fetching in the most curious out-of-the-way things to show them.

"My pretty shaving," said Martin proudly.

When they looked they were amazed and horrified to see a spotted green snake coiled comfortably up in the pinafore. It didn't appear to like being looked at by them, for it raised its curious heart-shaped head and flicked its little red, forked tongue at them.

His mother gave a great scream, and dropped the jug she had in her hand upon the floor, while John rushed off to get a big stick. "Drop it, Martin —drop the wicked snake before it stings you, and I'll soon kill it."

Martin stared, surprised at the fuss they were making; then, still tightly holding the ends of his pinafore, he turned and ran out of the room and away as fast as he could go. Away went his father after him, stick in hand, and out of the gate into the thicket of tall wild sunflowers where Martin had vanished from sight. After hunting about for some time, he found the little runaway sitting on the ground among the weeds.

"Where's the snake?" he cried.

"Gone!" said Martin, waving his little hand around. "I let it go and you mustn't look for it."

John picked the child up in his arms and marched

back to the room and popped him down on the floor, then gave him a good scolding. "It's a mercy the poisonous thing didn't sting you," he said. "You're a naughty little boy to play with snakes, because they're dangerous bad things, and you die if they bite you. And now you must go straight to bed; that's the only punishment that has any effect on such a harebrained little butterfly."

Martin, puckering up his face for a cry, crept away to his little room. It was very hard to have to go to bed in the daytime when he was not sleepy, and when the birds and butterflies were out in the sunshine having such a good time.

"It's not a bit of use scolding him—I found that out long ago," said Mrs. John, shaking her head. "Do you know, John, I can't help thinking sometimes that he's not our child at all."

"Whose child do you think he is, then?" said John, who had a cup of water in his hand, for the chase after Martin had made him hot, and he wanted cooling.

"I don't know—but I once had a very curious dream."

"People often do have curious dreams," said wise old John.

"But this was a very curious one, and I remember saying to myself: If this doesn't mean something that is going to happen, then dreams don't count for much."

"No more they do," said John.

"It was in England, just when we were getting

ready for the voyage, and it was autumn, when the birds were leaving us. I dreamed that I went out alone and walked by the sea, and stood watching a great number of swallows flying by and out over the sea—flying away to some distant land. By-and-by I noticed one bird coming down lower and lower as if he wanted to alight, and I watched it, and it came down straight to me, and at last flew right into my bosom. I put my hand on it, and looking close saw that it was a martin, all pure white on its throat and breast, and with a white patch on its back. Then I woke up, and it was because of that dream that I named our child Martin, instead of John as you wished to do. Now when I watch swallows flying about, coming and going round the house, I sometimes think that Martin came to us like that one in the dream, and that some day he will fly away from us. When he gets bigger, I mean."

"When he gets littler, you mean," said John with a laugh. "No, no, he's too big for a swallow—a Michaelmas goose would be nothing to him for size. But here I am listening to your silly dreams instead of watering the melons and cucumbers!" And out he went to his garden, but in a minute he put his head in at the door and said, "You may go and tell him to get up if you like. Poor little fellow! Only make him promise not to go chumming with spotted snakes any more, and not to bring them into the house, because somehow they disagree with me."

CHAPTER II

THE SPOONBILL AND THE CLOUD

AS Martin grew in years and strength, his age being now about seven, his rambles began to extend beyond the waste grounds outside of the fenced orchard and gate. These waste grounds were a wilderness of weeds: here were the sunflowers that Martin liked best; the wild cock's-comb, flaunting great crimson tufts; the yellow flowering mustard, taller than the tallest man; giant thistle, and wild pumpkin with spotted leaves; the huge hairy fox-gloves with yellow bells; feathery fennel, and the big grey green thorn-apples, with prickly burs full of bright red seed, and long white wax-like flowers, that bloomed only in the evening. He could never get high enough on anything to see over the tops of these plants; but at last he found his way through them, and discovered, on their further side, a wide grassy plain with scarcely a tree on it, stretching away into the blue distance. On this vast plain he gazed with wonderment and delight. Behind the orchard and weedy waste the ground sloped down to a stream of running water, full of tall rushes with dark-green polished stems, and yellow water-lilies. All along the moist banks grew other flowers that were never seen in the dry ground above—the blue star, and scarlet and white

7

verbenas; and sweet peas of all colours; and the
delicate red vinegar flower, and angel's hair, and the
small fragrant lilies called Mary's-tears, and tall
scattered flags, flaunting their yellow blossoms high
above the meadow grass.

Every day Martin ran down to the stream to
gather flowers and shells; for many curious water-
snails were found there with brown purple-striped
shells; and he also liked to watch the small birds
that build their nests in the rushes.

There were three of these small birds that did not
appear to know that Martin loved them; for no
sooner would he present himself at the stream than
forth they would flutter in a great state of mind.
One, the prettiest, was a tiny, green-backed little
creature, with a crimson crest and a velvet-black
band across a bright yellow breast: this one had a
soft, low, complaining voice, clear as a silver bell.
The second was a brisk little grey-and-black fellow,
with a loud, indignant chuck, and a broad tail which
he incessantly opened and shut, like a Spanish lady
playing with her fan. The third was a shy, mysterious
little brown bird, peering out of the clustering leaves,
and making a sound like the soft ticking of a clock.
They were like three little men, an Italian, a Dutch-
man, and a Hindoo, talking together, each in his
own language, and yet well able to understand
each other. Martin could not make out what they
said, but suspected that they were talking about
him; and he feared that their remarks were not
always of a friendly nature.

At length he made the discovery that the water of the stream was perpetually running away. If he dropped a leaf on the surface it would hasten down stream, and toss about and fret impatiently against anything that stood in its way, until, making its escape, it would quickly hurry out of sight. Whither did this rippling, running water go? He was anxious to find out. At length, losing all fear and fired with the sight of many new and pretty things he found while following it, he ran along the banks, until, miles from home, he came to a great lake he could hardly see across, it was so broad. It was a wonderful place, full of birds; not small, fretful creatures flitting in and out of the rushes, but great, majestic birds that took very little notice of him. Far out on the blue surface of the water floated numbers of wild fowl, and chief among them for grace and beauty was the swan, pure white with black head and neck and crimson bill. There also were stately flamingoes, stalking along knee-deep in the water, which was shallow; and nearer to the shore were flocks of rose-coloured spoonbills and solitary big grey herons standing motionless; also groups of white egrets, and a great multitude of glossy ibises, with dark-green and purple plumage and long sickle-like beaks.

The sight of this water with its beds of rushes and tall flowering reeds, and its great company of birds, filled Martin with delight; and other joys were soon to follow. Throwing off his shoes, he dashed with a shout into the water, frightening a number of ibises; up they flew, each bird uttering a cry repeated many times, that sounded just like his old father's laugh when he laughed loud and heartily. Then what was Martin's amazement to hear his own shout and this chorus of bird ha, ha, ha's, repeated by hundreds of voices all over the lake. At first he thought that the other birds were mocking the ibises; but presently he shouted again, and again his shouts were repeated by dozens of voices. This delighted him so much that he spent the whole day shouting himself hoarse at the waterside.

When he related his wonderful experience at home, and heard from his father that the sounds he had heard were only echoes from the beds of rushes, he was not a bit wiser than before, so that the echoes remained to him a continual wonder and source of never-failing pleasure.

Every day he would take some noisy instrument to the lake to startle the echoes; a whistle his father made him served for a time; after that he marched up and down the banks, rattling a tin canister with pebbles in it; then he got a large frying-pan from the kitchen, and beat on it with a stick every day for about a fortnight. When he grew tired of all these sounds, and began casting about for some new thing to wake the echoes with, he all at once remembered his father's gun—just what he wanted, for it was the noisiest thing in the world. Watching his opportunity, he got secretly into the room where it was kept loaded, and succeeded in carrying it out of the house without being seen; then, full of joyful anticipations, he ran as fast as the heavy gun would let him to his favourite haunt.

When he arrived at the lake, three or four spoon-bills—those beautiful, tall, rose-coloured birds—were standing on the bank, quietly dozing in the hot sun-shine. They did not fly away at his approach, for the birds were now so accustomed to Martin and his harmless noises that they took very little notice of him. He knelt on one knee and pointed the gun at them.

"Now birdies, you don't know what a fright I'm going to give you—off you go!" he cried, and pulled the trigger.

The roar of the loud report travelled all over the wide lake, creating a great commotion among the feathered people, and they rose up with a general scream into the air.

All this was of no benefit to Martin, the recoil of the gun having sent him flying over, his heels in the air; and before he recovered himself the echoes were silent, and all the frightened birds were settling on the water again. But there, just before him, lay one of the spoonbills, beating its great rose-coloured wings against the ground.

Martin ran to it full of keen distress, but was powerless to help; its life's blood was fast running away from the shot-wounds it had received in its side, staining the grass with crimson. Presently it closed its beautiful ruby-coloured eyes and the quivering wings grew still.

Then Martin sat down on the grass by its side and began to cry. Oh, that great bird, half as tall as himself, and so many times more lovely and strong and beautiful in its life—he had killed it, and it would never fly again! He raised it up very tenderly in his arms and kissed it—kissed its pale green head and rosy wings; then out of his arms it tumbled back again on to the grass.

"Oh, poor bird," he cried suddenly, "open your wings and fly away!"

But it was dead.

Then Martin got up and stared all round him at the wide landscape, and everything looked strange and dim and sorrowful. A shadow passed over the lake, and a murmur came up out of the rushes that was like a voice saying something that he could not understand. A great cry of pain rose from his heart and died to a whisper on his lips; he was awed into silence. Sinking down upon the grass again, he hid his face against the rosy-breasted bird and began to sob. How warm the dead bird felt against his cheek—oh, so warm—and it could not live and fly about with the others.

At length he sat up and knew the reason of that change that had come over the earth. A dark cloud had sprung up in the south-west, far off as yet, and near the horizon; but its fringe already touched and obscured the low-hanging sun, and a shadow flew far and vast before it. Over the lake flew that great shadow: the waters looked cold and still, reflecting as in a polished glass the motionless rushes, the grassy bank, and Martin, sitting on it, still clasping in his arms the dead rose-coloured bird.

Swifter and vaster, following close upon the flying shadow, came the mighty cloud, changing from black to slaty grey; and then, as the sun broke forth again under its lower edge, it was all flushed with a brilliant rose colour. But what a marvellous thing it was, when the cloud covered a third of the wide heavens, almost touching the horizon on either side with its wing-like extremities; Martin gazing steadily at it, saw that in its form it was like an immense spoonbill flying through the air! He would gladly have run away then, to hide himself from its sight, but he dared not stir, for it was now directly above him; so, lying down on the grass and hiding his face against the dead bird, he waited in fear and trembling.

He heard the rushing sound of the mighty wings: the wind they created smote on the waters in a hurricane, so that the reeds were beaten flat on the surface, and a great cry of terror went up from all the wild birds. It passed, and when Martin raised his bowed head and looked again, the sun, just about to touch the horizon with its great red globe, shone out, shedding a rich radiance over the earth and water; while far off, on the opposite side of the heavens, the great cloud-bird was rapidly fading out of sight.

CHAPTER III

AFTER what had happened Martin could never visit the waterside and look at the great birds wading and swimming there without a feeling that was like a sudden coldness in the blood of his veins. The rosy spoonbill he had killed and cried over and the great bird-cloud that had frightened him were never forgotten. He grew tired of shouting to the echoes: he discovered that there were even more wonderful things than the marsh echoes in the world, and that the world was bigger than he had thought it. When spring with its moist verdure and frail, sweet-smelling flowers had gone; when the great plain began to turn to a rusty-brown colour, and the dry hard earth was full of cracks, and the days grew longer and the heat greater, there came an appearance of water that quivered and glittered and danced before his wondering sight, and would lead him miles from home every day in his vain efforts to find out what it was. He could talk of nothing else, and asked endless questions about it, and they told him that this strange thing was nothing but the Mirage, but of course that was not telling him enough, so that he was left to puzzle his little-boy brains over this new mystery, just as

14

they had puzzled before over the mystery of the echoes. Now, this Mirage was a glittering whiteness that looked just like water, always shining and dancing before him and all round him, on the dry level plain where there was no water. It was never quiet, but perpetually quivering and running into wavelets that threw up crests and jets of sprays as from a fountain, and showers of brilliant drops that flashed like molten silver in the sunlight before they broke and vanished, only to be renewed again. It appeared every day when the sun was high and the air hot, and it was often called *The False Water*. And false it was, since it always flew before him as he ran, so that although he often seemed to be getting nearer to it he could never quite overtake it. But Martin had a very determined spirit for a small boy, and although this appearance of water mocked his efforts a hundred times every day with its vanishing brightness and beauty, he would not give up the pursuit.

Now, one day when there was not a cloud on the great hot whitey-blue sky, nor a breath of air stirring, when it was all silent, for not even a grasshopper creaked in the dead, yellow, motionless grass, the whole level earth began to shine and sparkle like a lake of silvery water, as Martin had never seen it shine before. He had wandered far away from home —never had he been so far—and still he ran and ran and ran, and still that whiteness quivered and glittered and flew on before him; and ever it looked more tempt-ingly near, urging him to fresh exertions. At length, tired out and overcome with heat, he sat down to

rest, and feeling very much hurt at the way he had
been deceived and led on, he shed one little tear.
There was no mistake about that tear; he felt it
running like a small spider down his cheek, and finally
he saw it fall. It fell on to a blade of yellow grass and
ran down the blade, then stopped so as to gather
itself into a little round drop before touching the
ground. Just then, out of the roots of the grass
beneath it, crept a tiny dusty black beetle and began
drinking the drop, waving its little horns up and
down like donkey's ears, apparently very much
pleased at its good fortune in finding water and
having a good drink in such a dry, thirsty place.
Probably it took the tear for a drop of rain just fallen
out of the sky.

"You *are* a funny little thing!" exclaimed Martin,
feeling now less like crying than laughing.

The wee beetle, satisfied and refreshed, climbed
up the grass-blade, and when it reached the tip
lifted its dusty-black wing-cases just enough to
throw out a pair of fine gauzy wings that had been
neatly folded up beneath them, and flew away.

Martin, following its flight, had his eyes quite
dazzled by the intense glitter of the False Water,
which now seemed to be only a few yards from
him: but the strangest thing was that in it there
appeared a form — a bright beautiful form that
vanished when he gazed steadily at it. Again he
got up and began running harder than ever after
the flying mocking Mirage, and every time he stopped
he fancied that he could see the figure again, some-

times like a pale blue shadow on the brightness, sometimes shining with its own excessive light, and sometimes only seen in outline, like a figure graved on glass, and always vanishing when looked at steadily. Perhaps that white water-like glitter of the Mirage was like a looking-glass, and he was only chasing his own reflection. I cannot say, but there it was, always before him, a face as of a beautiful boy, with tumbled hair and laughing lips, its figure clothed in a fluttering dress of lights and shadows. It also seemed to beckon to him with its hand, and encourage him to run on after it with its bright merry glances.

At length when it was past the hour of noon, Martin sat down under a small bush that gave just shade enough to cover him and none to spare. It was only a little spot of shade like an island in a sea of heat and brightness. He was too hot and tired to run more, too tired even to keep his eyes open, and so, propping his back against the stem of the small bush, he closed his tired hot eyes.

B

CHAPTER IV

MARTIN kept his eyes shut for only about a minute, as he thought; but he must have been asleep some time, for when he opened them the False Water had vanished, and the sun, looking very large and crimson, was just about to set. He started up, feeling very thirsty and hungry and bewildered; for he was far, far from home, and lost on the great plain. Presently he spied a man coming towards him on horseback. A very funny-looking old man he proved to be, with a face wrinkled and tanned by sun and wind, until it resembled a piece of ancient shoe-leather left lying for years on some neglected spot of ground. A Brazil nut is not darker nor more wrinkled than was the old man's face. His long matted beard and hair had once been white, but the sun out of doors and the smoke in his smoky hut had given them a yellowish tinge, so that they looked like dry dead grass. He wore big jack-boots, patched all over, and full of cracks and holes; and a great pea-jacket, rusty and ragged, fastened with horn buttons big as saucers. His old brimless hat looked like a dilapidated tea-cosy on his head, and to prevent it from being carried off by the wind it was kept on with an old flannel shirt-sleeve tied under his chin. His saddle, too, like his clothes, was old and full of rents, with wisps of hair and straw stuffing sticking out in various places, and his feet were thrust into a pair of big stirrups made of pieces of wood and rusty iron tied together with string and wire.

"Boy, what may you be a-doing of here?" bawled this old man at the top of his voice: for he was as deaf as a post, and like a good many deaf people thought it necessary to speak very loud to make himself heard.

"Playing," answered Martin innocently. But he could not make the old man hear until he stood up on tip-toe and shouted out his answer as loud as he could.

"Playing!" exclaimed the old man. "Well, I never in all my life! When there ain't a house 'cepting my own for leagues and leagues, and he says he's playing! What may you be, now?" he shouted again.

"A little boy," screamed Martin.

"I knowed that afore I axed," said the other. Then he slapped his legs and held up his hands with astonishment, and at last began to chuckle. "Will you come home along o' me?" he shouted.

"Will you give me something to eat?" asked Martin in return.

"Haw, haw, haw!" guffawed the old fellow. It was a tremendous laugh, so loud and hollow, it astonished and almost frightened Martin to hear it. "Well I never!" he said. "He ain't no fool, neither.

Now old Jacob, just you take your time and think a bit afore you makes your answer to that."

This curious old man, whose name was Jacob, had lived so long by himself that he always thought out loud—louder than other people talk: for, being deaf, he could not hear himself, and never had a suspicion that he could be heard by others.

"He's lost, that's what he is," continued old Jacob aloud to himself. "And what's more he's been and gone and forgot all about his own home, and all he wants is summat to eat. I'll take him and keep him, that's what I'll do: for he's a stray lamb, and belongs to him that finds him, like any other lamb I finds. I'll make him believe I'm his old dad; for he's little and will believe most anythink you tells him. I'll learn him to do things about the house— to boil the kettle, and cook the wittels, and gather the firewood, and mend the clothes, and do the washing, and draw the water, and milk the cow, and dig the potatoes, and mind the sheep and—and—and that's what I'll learn him. Then, Jacob, you can sit down and smoke your pipe, 'cos you'll have someone to do your work for you."

Martin stood quietly listening to all this, not quite understanding the old man's kind intentions. Then old Jacob, promising to give him something to eat, pulled him up on to his horse, and started home at a gallop.

Soon they arrived at a mud hovel, thatched with rushes, the roof sloping down so low that one could almost step on to it; it was surrounded with a ditch, and had a potato patch and a sheep enclosure; for old Jacob was a shepherd, and had a flock of sheep. There were several big dogs, and when Martin got down from the horse, they began jumping round him, barking with delight, as if they knew him, half-smothering him with their rough caresses. Jacob led him into the hut, which looked extremely dirty and neglected, and had only one room. In the corners against the walls were piles of sheep-skins that had a strong and rather unpleasant smell: the thatch above was covered with dusty cobwebs, hanging like old rags, and the clay floor was littered with bones, sticks, and other rubbish. The only nice thing to see was a tea - kettle singing and steaming away merrily on the fire in the grate. Old Jacob set about preparing the evening meal; and soon they sat down at a small deal table to a supper of cold mutton and potatoes, and tea which did not taste very nice, as it was sweetened with moist black sugar. Martin was too hungry to turn up his nose at anything, and while he ate and drank the old man chuckled and talked aloud to himself about his good fortune in finding a little boy to do his work for him. After supper he cleared the table, and put two mugs of tea on it, and then got out his clay pipe and tobacco.

"Now, little boy," he cried, "let's have a jolly evening together. Your very good health, little boy," and here he jingled his mug against Martin's, and took a sip of tea.

"Would you like to hear a song, little boy?" he said, after finishing his pipe.

"No," said Martin, who was getting sleepy; but
Jacob took " no " to mean "yes," and so he stood up
on his legs and sang this song:

> My name is Jacob, that's my name;
> And tho' I'm old, the old man's game—
> The air it is so good, d'ye see:
> And on the plain my flock I keep,
> And sing all day to please my sheep,
> And never lose them like Bo-Peep,
> Becos the ways of them are known to me.
>
> When winter comes and winds do blow,
> Unto my sheep so good I go—
> I'm always good to them, d'ye see—
> Ho, sheep, say I, both ram and ewe,
> I've sung you songs all summer through,
> Now lend to me a skin or two,
> To keep the cold and wet from out o' me.

This song, accompanied with loud raps on the table,
was bellowed forth in a dreadfully discordant voice;
and very soon all the dogs rushed into the room and
began to bark and howl most dismally, which seemed
to please the old man greatly, for to him it was a
kind of applause. But the noise was too much for
Martin; so he stopped up his ears, and only removed
his fingers from them when the performance was over.
After the song the old man offered to dance, for he
had not yet had amusement enough.

"Boy, can you play on this?" he shouted, holding
up a frying-pan and a big stick to beat it with.

Of course Martin could play on that instrument:
he had often enough played on one like it to startle
the echoes on the lake, in other days. And so, when
he had been lifted on to the table, he took the frying-

pan by the handle, and began vigorously beating on it with the stick. He did not mind the noise now, since he was helping to make it. Meanwhile old Jacob began flinging his arms and legs about in all directions, looking like a scarecrow made to tumble about by means of springs and wires. He pounded the clay floor with his ponderous old boots until the room was filled with a cloud of dust; then in his excitement he kicked over chairs, pots, kettles, and whatever came in his way, while he kept on revolving round the table in a kind of crazy fandango. Martin thought it fine fun, and screamed with laughter, and beat his gong louder than ever; then to make matters worse old Jacob at intervals uttered whoops and yells, which the dogs answered with long howls from the door, until the din was something tremendous.

At length they both grew tired, and then after resting and sipping some more cold tea, prepared to go to bed. Some sheep-skins were piled up in a corner for Martin to sleep on, and old Jacob covered him with a horse-rug, and tucked him in very carefully. Then the kind old man withdrew to his own bed on the opposite side of the room.

About midnight Martin was wakened by loud, horrible noises in the room, and started up in bed trembling with fear. The sounds came from the old man's nose, and resembled a succession of blasts on a ram's horn which, on account of its roughness and twisted shape, makes a very bad trumpet. As soon as Martin discovered the cause of the noise he crept out of bed and tried to waken the old snorer by shouting at him, tugging at his arms and legs, and finally pulling his beard. He refused to wake. Then Martin had a bright idea, and groping his way to the bucket of cold water standing beside the fireplace, he managed to raise it up in his arms, and poured it over the sleeper.

The snoring changed to a series of loud choking snorts, then ceased. Martin, well pleased at the success of his experiment, was about to return to his bed when old Jacob struggled up to a sitting posture.

"Hullo, wake up, little boy!" he shouted. "My bed's all full o' water—goodness knows where it comes from."

"I poured it over you to wake you up. Don't you know you were making a noise with your nose?" cried Martin at the top of his voice.

"You—you—you throwed it over me! You—O you most wicked little villain, you! You throwed it over me, did you!" and here he poured out such a torrent of abusive words that Martin was horrified and cried out, "O what a naughty, wicked, bad old man you are!"

It was too dark for old Jacob to see him, but he knew his way about the room, and taking up the wet rug that served him for covering he groped his way to Martin's bed and began pounding it with the rug, thinking the naughty little boy was there.

"You little rascal, you—I hope you like that!— and that!—and that!" he shouted, pounding away. "I'll learn you to throw water over your poor old dad! And such a—a affectionate father as I've been too, giving him sich nice wittels, and—and singing and dancing to him to teach him music. Perhaps you'd like a little more, you takes it so quietly? Well, then, take that!—and that!—and that! Why, how's this—the young warmint ain't here arter all! Well, I'm blowed if that don't beat everythink! What did he go and chuck that water over me for? What a walloping I'll give him in the morning when it's light! and now, boy, you may go and sleep on my bed, 'cos it's wet, d'ye see; and I'll sleep on yourn, 'cos it's dry."

Then he got into Martin's bed, and muttered and grumbled himself to sleep. Martin came out from under the table, and after dressing himself with great secrecy crept to the door to make his escape. It was locked and the key taken away. But he was determined to make his escape somehow, and not wait to be whipped; so, by-and-by, he drew the little deal table close against the wall, and getting on to it began picking the rushes one by one out of the lower part of the thatch. After working for half an hour, like a mouse eating his way out of a soft wooden box, he began to see the light coming through the hole, and in another half-hour it was large enough for him to creep through. When he had got out, he slipped down to the ground, where the dogs were lying. They seemed very glad to see him, and began pressing round to lick his face; but he pushed them off, and ran away over the plain as fast as he could. The stars were shining, but it was very dark and silent; only in moist places, where the grass grew tall, he heard the crickets strumming sadly on their little harps.

At length, tired with running, he coiled himself in a large tussock of dry grass and went to sleep, just as if he had been accustomed to sleep out of doors all his life.

CHAPTER V

IN that remote land where Martin was born, with its bright warm climate and rich soil, no person need go very long hungry—not even a small boy alone and lost on the great grassy plain. For there is a little useful plant in that place, with small leaves like clover leaves and a pretty yellow flower, which bears a wholesome sweet root, about as big as a pigeon's egg and of a pearly white colour. It is so well known to the settlers' children in that desert country that they are always wandering off to the plain to look for it, just as the children in a town are always running off with their halfpence to the sweet-stuff shop. This pretty white root is watery, so that it satisfies both hunger and thirst at the same time. Now when Martin woke next morning, he found a great many of the little three-leaved plants growing close to the spot where he had slept, and they supplied him with a nice sweet breakfast. After he had eaten enough and had amused himself by rolling over and over several times on the grass, he started once more on his travels, going towards the sunrise as fast as he could run. He could run well for a small boy, but he got tired at last, and sat down to rest. Then he jumped up and went on again at a trot:

this pace he kept up very steadily, only pausing from time to time to watch a flock of small white birds that followed him all the morning out of curiosity. At length he began to feel so hot and tired that he could only walk. Still he kept on; he could see no flowers nor anything pretty in that place—why should he stay in it? He would go on, and on, and on, in spite of the heat, until he came to something. But it grew hotter as the day advanced, and the ground about him more dry and barren and desolate, until at last he came to ground where there was scarcely a blade of grass: it was a great, barren, level plain, covered with a slight crust of salt crystals that glittered in the sun so brightly that it dazzled and pained his eyesight. Here were no sweet watery roots for refreshment, and no berries; nor could Martin find a bush to give him a little shade and protection from the burning noonday sun. He saw one large dark object in the distance, and mistaking it for a bush covered with thick foliage he ran towards it; but suddenly it started up, when he was near, and waving its great grey and white wings like sails, fled across the plain. It was an ostrich!

Now this hot, shadeless plain seemed to be the very home and dwelling-place of the False Water. It sparkled and danced all round him so close that there only appeared to be a small space of dry ground for him to walk on; only he was always exactly in the centre of the dry spot; for as he advanced, the glittering whiteness that looked so like shiny water, flew mockingly before his steps. But he hoped to

get to it at last, as every time he flagged in the chase
the mysterious figure of the day before appeared
again to lure him still further on. At length, unable
to move another step, Martin sat right down on the
bare ground: it was like sitting on the floor of a
heated oven, but there was no help for it, he was so
tired. The air was so thick and heavy that he could
hardly breathe, even with his mouth wide open like
a little gasping bird; and the sky looked like metal,
heated to a white heat, and so low down as to make
him fancy that if he were to throw up his hands he
would touch it and burn his fingers.

And the Mirage—oh, how it glistened and quivered
here where he had sat down, half blinding him with
its brightness! Now that he could no longer run
after it, nor even walk, it came to him, breaking
round and over him in a thousand fantastic shapes,
filling the air with a million white flakes that whirled
about as if driven by a furious wind, although not
a breath was stirring. They looked like whitest
snow-flakes, yet stung his cheeks like sparks of fire.
Not only did he see and feel, he could even *hear*
it now: his ears were filled with a humming sound,
growing louder and louder every minute, like the
noise made by a large colony of bumble-bees when
a person carelessly treads on their nest, and they are
angered and thrown into a great commotion and
swarm out to defend their home. Very soon out of
this confused murmur louder, clearer sounds began
to rise; and these could be distinguished as the
notes of numberless musical instruments and voices

of people singing, talking, and laughing. Then, all at once, there appeared running and skipping over the ground towards him a great company of girls—scores and hundreds of them scattered over the plain, exceeding in loveliness all lovely things that he had ever beheld. Their faces were whiter than lilies, and their loose, fluttering hair looked like a mist of pale shining gold; and their skirts, that rustled as they ran, were also shining like the wings of dragon-flies, and were touched with brown reflections and changing, beautiful tints, such as are seen on soap-bubbles. Each of them carried a silver pitcher, and as they ran and skipped along they dipped their fingers in and sprinkled the desert with water. The bright drops they scattered fell all around in a grateful shower, and flew up again from the heated earth in the form of a white mist touched with rainbow colours, filling the air with a refreshing coolness.

At Martin's side there grew a small plant, its grey-green leaves lying wilted on the ground, and one of the girls paused to water it, and as she sprinkled the drops on it she sang:

> Little weed, little weed,
>   In such need,
> Must you pain, ask in vain,
>   Die for rain,
> Never bloom, never seed,
>   Little weed?
> O, no, no, you shall not die,
>   From the sky
> With my pitcher down I fly.
> Drink the rain, grow again,
>   Bloom and seed,
>   Little weed.

Martin held up his hot little hands to catch some of the falling drops; then the girl, raising her pitcher, poured a stream of cool water right into his face, and laughing at what she had done, went away with a hop, skip, and jump after her companions.

The girls with pitchers had all gone, and were succeeded by troops of boys, just as beautiful, many of them singing and some playing on wind and stringed instruments; and some were running, others quietly walking, and still others riding on various animals—ostriches, sheep, goats, fawns, and small donkeys, all pure white. One boy was riding on a ram, and as he came by, strum-strumming on a little silver-stringed banjo, he sang a very curious song, which made Martin prick up his ears to listen. It was about a speckled snake that lived far away on a piece of waste ground; how day after day he sought for his lost playmate—the little boy that had left him; how he glided this way and that on his smooth, bright belly, winding in and out among the tall wild sunflowers; how he listened for the dear footsteps—listened with his green leaf-shaped, little head raised high among the leaves. But his playmate was far away and came no more to feed him from his basin of bread and milk, and caress his cold, smooth coils with his warm, soft, little hand.

Close after the boy on the ram marched four other little boys on foot, holding up long silver trumpets in readiness to blow. One of them stopped, and putting his trumpet down close to Martin's ear, puffed out his little round cheeks, and blew a blast that made him jump. Laughing at the joke, they passed on, and were succeeded by others and still others, singing, shouting, twanging their instruments, and some of them stopping for a few moments to look at Martin or play some pretty little trick on him.

But now all at once Martin ceased to listen or even look at them, for something new and different was coming, something strange which made him curious and afraid at the same time. It was a sound, very deep and solemn, of men's voices singing together a song that was like a dirge and coming nearer and nearer, and it was like the coming of a storm with wind and rain and thunder. Soon he could see them marching through the great crowd of people—old men moving in a slow procession, and they had pale dark faces and their hair and long beards were whiter than snow, and their long flowing robes were of the silvery dark colour of a rain-cloud. Then he saw that the leaders of the procession were followed by others who carried a couch of mother-o'-pearl resting on their shoulders, that on the couch reposed a pale sweet-looking youth dressed in silk clothes of a delicate rose-colour. He also wore crimson shoes, and a tight-fitting apple-green skull cap, which made his head look very small. His eyes were ruby-red, and he had a long slender nose like a snipe's bill, only broad and flattened at the tip. And then Martin saw that he was wounded, for he had one white hand pressed to his side and it was stained with blood, and drops of blood were trickling through his fingers.

He was troubled at the sight, and he gazed at him, and listened to the words of that solemn song the old men were singing but could not understand them. Not because he was a child, for no person, however aged and wise and filled with all learning he might be, could have understood that strange song about Wonderful Life and Wonderful Death. Yet there was something in it too which anyone who heard it, man or child, could understand; and he understood it, and it went into his heart to make it so heavy and sad that he could have put his little face down on the ground and cried as he had never cried before. But he did not put his face down and cry, for just then the wounded youth looked down on him as they carried him past and smiled a very sweet smile: then Martin felt that he loved him above all the bright and beautiful beings that had passed before him.

Then, when he was gone from sight; when the solemn sound of the voices began to grow fainter in the distance like the sound of a storm when it passes away, his heaviness of heart and sorrow left him, and he began to listen to the shouts and cries and clanging of noisy instruments of music swiftly coming nearer and nearer; and then all round and past him came a vast company of youths and maidens singing and playing and shouting and dancing as they moved onwards. They were the most beautiful beings he had ever seen in their shining dresses, some all in white, others in amber-colour, others in sky-blue, and some in still other lovely colours. "The

c

Queen! the Queen!" they were shouting. "Stand up, little boy, and bow to the Queen."

"The Queen! Kneel to the Queen, little boy," cried others.

Then many others in the company began crying out together, "The Queen! lie down flat on the ground, little boy."

"The Queen! Shut your eyes and open your mouth, little boy."

"The Queen! Run away as fast as you can, little boy."

"Stand on your head to the Queen, little boy!"

"Crow like a cock and bark like a dog, little boy!"

Trying to obey all these conflicting commands at one and the same time, poor Martin made strange noises and tumbled about this way and that and set them all laughing at him.

"The Queen wishes to speak to you—stand up, little boy," said one of the brightest beings, touching Martin on the cheek.

There before him, surrounded by all that beautiful company, stood the horses that drew her—great milk-white horses impatiently pawing the dusty ground with their hoofs and proudly champing their gold bridles, tossing the white froth from their mouths. But when he lifted his eyes timidly to the majestic being seated in her chariot before him he was dazzled and overcome with the sight. Her face had a brightness that was like that of the Mirage at noon, and the eyes that gazed on him were like two great opals; she appeared clothed in a white shining mist, and her

hair spread wide on her shoulders looked white—
whiter than a lamb's fleece, and powdered with fine
gold that sparkled and quivered and ran through it
like sparks of yellow fire: and on her head she wore
a crown that was like a diamond seen by candle-
light, or like a dewdrop in the sun, and every moment
it changed its colour, and by turns was a red flame,
then a green, then a yellow, then a violet.

"Child, you have followed me far," said the Queen,
"and now you are rewarded, for you have looked on
my face, and I have refreshed you; and the Sun, my
father, will never more hurt you for my sake."

"He is a naughty boy and unworthy of your
goodness," spoke one of the bright beings standing
near. "He killed the spoonbill."

"He cried for the poor slain bird," replied the
Queen. "He will never remember it without grief,
and I forgive him."

"He went away from his home and thinks no more
of his poor old father and mother, who cry for him
and are seeking for him on the great plain," continued
the voice.

"I forgive him," returned the Queen. "He is
such a little wanderer—he could not always rest
at home."

"He emptied a bucketful of water over good old
Jacob, who found him and took him in and fed him,
and sang to him, and danced to him, and was a
second father to him."

At that there was great laughter; even the Queen
laughed when she said that she forgave him that too.

And Martin when he remembered old Jacob, and saw
that they only made a joke of it, laughed with them.
But the accusing voice still went on:

"And when the good old shepherd went to sleep
a second time, then the naughty little boy climbed
on the table and picked a hole in the thatch and got
out and ran away."

Another burst of laughter followed; then a youth
in a shining, violet - coloured dress suddenly began
twanging on his instrument and wildly capering about
in imitation of old Jacob's dancing, and while he
played and danced he sang:

Ho, sheep whose ways are known to me,
Both ewe and lamb
And horned ram,
Wherever can that Martin be?
All day for him I ride
Over the plains so wide,
And on my horn I blow,
Just to let him know
That Jacob's on his track,
And soon will have him back,
I look and look all day,
And when I'm home I say:
He isn't like a mole
To dig himself a hole;
Them little legs he's got
They can't go far, trot, trot,
They can't go far, run, run,
Oh no, it is his fun;
I'm sure he's near,
He must be here
A-skulking round the house
Just like a little mouse.
I'll get a mouse-trap in a minute,
And bait with cheese that's smelly
To bring him helter-skelly—
That little empty belly,
And then I'll have him in it.

Where have he hid,
That little kid,
That good old Jacob was so kind to?
And when a rest I am inclined to
Who'll boil the cow and dig the kittles
And milk the stockings, darn the wittles?
Who mugs of tea
Will drink with me?
When round and round
I pound the ground
With boots of cowhide, boots of thunder,
Who'll help to make the noise, I wonder?
Who'll join the row
Of loud bow-wow
With din of tin and copper clatter,
With bang and whang of pan and platter?
O when I find
Him fast I'll bind
And upside down I'll hold him;
And when a-home I gallop late-o
I'll give him no more cold potato,
But cuff him, box him, bang him, scold him,
And drench him with a pail of water,
And fill his mouth with wool and mortar,
Because he don't do things he oughter,
But does the things he ought not to,
Then tell me true,
Both ram and ewe,
Wherever have that Martin got to?
For Jacob's old and deaf and dim,
And never knowed the ways of him.

"I forgive him everything," said the Queen very graciously, when the song ended, at which they all laughed. "And now let two of you speak and each bestow a gift on him. He deserves to be rewarded for running so far after us."

Then one of those bright beautiful beings came forward and cried out: "He loves wandering; let him have his will and be a wanderer all his days on the face of the earth."

"Well spoken!" cried the Queen.

"A wanderer he is to be," said another: "let the sea do him no harm—that is my gift."

"So be it," said the Queen; "and to your two gifts I shall add a third. Let all men love him. Go now, Martin, you are well equipped, and satisfy your heart with the sight of all the strange and beautiful things the world contains."

"Kneel and thank the Queen for her gifts," said a voice to Martin.

He dropped on to his knees, but could speak no word; when he raised his eyes again the whole glorious company had vanished.

The air was cool and fragrant, the earth moist as if a shower had just fallen. He got up and slowly walked onward until near sunset, thinking of nothing but the beautiful people of the Mirage. He had left the barren salt plain behind by now; the earth was covered with yellow grass, and he found and ate some sweet roots and berries. Then feeling very tired, he stretched himself out on his back and began to wonder if what he had seen was nothing but a dream. Yes, it was surely a dream, but then—in his life dreams and realities were so mixed—how was he always to know one from the other? Which was most strange, the Mirage that glittered and quivered round him and flew mockingly before him, or the people of the Mirage he had seen?

If you are lying quite still with your eyes shut and someone comes softly up and stands over you, somehow you know it, and open your eyes to see who it is. Just in that way Martin knew that someone had come and was standing over him. Still he kept his eyes shut, feeling sure that it was one of those bright and beautiful beings he had lately seen, perhaps the Queen herself, and that the sight of her shining countenance would dazzle his eyes. Then all at once he thought that it might be old Jacob, who would punish him for running away. He opened his eyes very quickly then. What do you think he saw? An ostrich—that same big ostrich he had seen and startled early in the day! It was standing over him, staring down with its great vacant eyes. Gradually its head came lower and lower down, until at last it made a sudden peck at a metal button on his jacket, and gave such a vigorous tug at it that Martin was almost lifted off the ground. He screamed and gave a jump; but it was nothing to the jump the ostrich gave when he discovered that the button belonged to a living boy. He jumped six feet high into the air and came down with a great flop; then feeling rather ashamed of himself for being frightened at such an insignificant thing as Martin, he stalked majestically away, glancing back, first over one shoulder then the other, and kicking up his heels behind him in a somewhat disdainful manner.

Martin laughed, and in the middle of his laugh he fell asleep.

CHAPTER VI

MARTIN MEETS WITH SAVAGES

WHEN, on waking next morning, Martin took his first peep over the grass, there, directly before him, loomed the great blue hills, or Sierras as they are called in that country. He had often seen them, long ago in his distant home on clear mornings, when they had appeared like a blue cloud on the horizon. He had even wished to get to them, to tread their beauitful blue summits that looked as if they would be soft to his feet—softer than the moist springy turf on the plain; but he wished it only as one wishes to get to some far-off impossible place —a white cloud, for instance, or the blue sky itself. Now all at once he unexpectedly found himself near them, and the sight fired him with a new desire. The level plain had nothing half so enchanting as the cloud-like blue airy hills, and very soon he was up on his feet and hurrying towards them. In spite of hurrying he did not seem to get any nearer; still it was pleasant to be always going on and on, knowing that he would get to them at last. He had now left the drier plains behind; the earth was clothed with green and yellow grass easy to the feet, and during the day he found many sweet roots to refresh him.

He also found quantities of cam-berries, a round fruit a little less than a cherry in size, bright yellow in colour, and each berry inside a green case or sheath shaped like a heart. They were very sweet. At night he slept once more in the long grass, and when daylight returned he travelled on, feeling very happy there alone—happy to think that he would get to the beautiful hills at last. But only in the early morning would they look distinct and near; later in the day, when the sun grew hot, they would seem further off, like a cloud resting on the earth, which made him think sometimes that they moved on as he went towards them.

On the third day he came to a high piece of ground; and when he got to the top and looked over to the other side he saw a broad green valley with a stream of water running in it; on one hand the valley with its gleaming water stretched away as far as he could see, or until it lost itself in the distant haze; but on the other hand, on looking up the valley, there appeared a great forest, looking blue in the distance; and this was the first forest that Martin had ever seen. Close by, down in the green valley before him, there was something else to attract his attention, and this was a large group of men and horses. No sooner had he caught sight of them than he set off at a run towards them, greatly excited; and as he drew near they all rose up from the grass where they had been sitting or lying to stare at him, filled with wonder at the sight of that small boy alone in the desert. There were about twenty men and women, and several children; the men were very big and tall, and were dressed only in robes made of the skins of some wild animal; they had broad, flat faces, and dark copper - coloured skins, and their long black hair hung down loose on their backs.

These strange, rude-looking people were savages, and are supposed to be cruel and wicked, and to take pleasure in torturing and killing any lost or stray person that falls into their hands; but indeed it is not so, as you shall shortly find. Poor ignorant little Martin, who had never read a book in his life, having always refused to learn his letters, knew nothing about savages, and feared them no more than he had feared old Jacob, or the small spotted snake, the very sight of which had made grown-up people scream and run away. So he marched boldly up and stared at them, and they in turn stared at him out of their great, dark, savage eyes.

They had just been eating their supper of deer's flesh, roasted on the coals, and after a time one of the savages, as an experiment, took up a bone of meat and offered it to him. Being very hungry he gladly took it, and began gnawing the meat off the bone.

When he had satisfied his hunger, he began to look round him, still stared at by the others. Then one of the women, who had a good-humoured face, caught him up, and seating him on her knees, tried to talk to him.

"Melu-melumia quiltahou papa shani cha silmata," she spoke, gazing very earnestly into his face.

They had all been talking among themselves while he was eating; but he did not know that savages had a language of their own different from ours, and so thought that they had only been amusing themselves with a kind of nonsense talk, which meant nothing. Now when the woman addressed this funny kind of talk to him, he answered her in her own way as he imagined, readily enough: "Hey diddle-diddle, the cat's in the fiddle, fe fo fi fum, chumpty-chumpty-chum, with bings on her ringers, and tells on her boes."

They all listened with grave attention, as if he had said something very important. Then the woman continued: "Huanatopa ana ana quiltahou."

To which Martin answered, "Theophilus Thistle, the thistle-sifter, sifted a sieve of unsifted thistles; and if Theophilus—oh, I won't say any more!"

Then she said, " Quira - holata silhoa mari changa changa."

"Cock-a-doodle-do!" cried Martin, getting tired and impatient. "Baa, baa, black sheep, bow, wow, wow; goosey, goosey gander; see-saw, Mary Daw; chick-a-dee-dee, will you listen to me. And now let me go!"

But she held him fast and kept on talking her nonsense language to him, until becoming vexed he caught hold of her hair and pulled it. She only laughed and tossed him up into the air and caught him again, just as he might have tossed and caught a small kitten. At length she released him, for now they were all beginning to lie down by the fire to sleep, as it was getting dark; Martin being very tired settled himself down among them, and as one of the women threw a skin over him he slept very comfortably.

Next morning the hills looked nearer than ever just across the river; but little he cared for hills now, and when the little savage children went out to hunt for berries and sweet roots he followed and spent the day agreeably enough in their company.

On the afternoon of the second day his new playfellows all threw off their little skin cloaks and plunged into the stream to bathe; and Martin, seeing how much they seemed to enjoy being in the water, undressed himself and went in after them. The water was not too deep in that place, and as it was rare fun splashing about and trying to keep his legs in the swift current and clambering over slippery rocks, he went out some distance from the bank. All at once he discovered that the others had left him, and looking back he saw that they were all scrambling out on to the bank and fighting over his clothes. Back he dashed in haste to rescue his property, but by the time he reached the spot they had finished dividing the spoil, and jumping up they ran away and scattered in all directions, one wearing his jacket, another his knickerbockers, another his shirt and one sock, another his cap and shoes, and the last the one remaining sock only. In vain he pursued and called after them; and at last he was compelled to follow them unclothed to the camping ground, where he presented himself crying piteously; but the women who had been so kind to him would not help him now, and only laughed to see how white his skin looked by contrast with the dark copper-coloured skins of the other children. At length one of them compassionately gave him a small soft-furred skin of some wild animal, and fastened it on him like a cloak; and this he was compelled to wear with shame and grief, feeling very strange and uncomfortable in it. But the feeling of discomfort in that new savage dress was nothing to the sense of injury that stung him, and in his secret heart he was determined not to lose his own clothes.

When the children went out next day he followed them, watching and waiting for a chance to recover anything that belonged to him; and at last, seeing the little boy who wore his cap off his guard, he made a sudden rush, and snatching it off the young savage's head, put it firmly upon his own. But the little savage now regarded that cap as his very own: he had taken it by force or stratagem, and had worn it on his head since the day before, and that made it his property; and so at Martin he went, and they fought stoutly together, and being nearly of a size, he could not conquer the little white boy. Then he cried out to the others to help him, and they came and overthrew Martin, and deprived him not only of his cap, but of his little skin cloak as well, and then punished him until he screamed aloud with pain. Leaving him crying on the ground, they ran back to the camp. He followed shortly afterwards, but got no sympathy, for, as a rule, grown-up savages do not trouble themselves very much about these little matters: they leave their children to settle their own disputes.

During the rest of that day Martin sulked by himself behind a great tussock of grass, refusing to eat with the others, and when one of the women went to him and offered him a piece of meat he struck it vindictively out of her hand. She only laughed a little and left him.

Now when the sun was setting, and he was beginning to feel very cold and miserable in his nakedness, the men were seen returning from the hunt; but instead of riding slowly to the camp as on other days, they came riding furiously and shouting. The moment they were seen and their shouts heard the women jumped up and began hastily packing the skins and all their belongings into bundles; and in less than ten minutes the whole company was mounted on horseback and ready for flight. One of the men picked Martin up and placed him on the horse's back before him, and then they all started at a swift canter up the valley towards that great blue forest in the distance.

In about an hour they came to it: it was then quite dark, the sky powdered with numberless stars; but when they got among the trees the blue, dusky sky and brilliant stars disappeared from sight, as if a black cloud had come over them, so dark was it in the forest. For the trees were very tall and mingled their branches overhead; but they had got into a narrow path known to them, and moving slowly in single file, they kept on for about two hours longer, then stopped and dismounted under the great trees, and lying down all close together, went to sleep. Martin, lying among them, crept under the edge of one of the large skin robes and, feeling warm, he soon fell fast asleep and did not wake till daylight.

CHAPTER VII

ALONE IN THE GREAT FOREST

IMAGINE to yourself one accustomed to live in the great treeless plain, accustomed to open his eyes each morning to the wide blue sky and the brilliant sunlight, now for the first time opening them in that vast gloomy forest, where neither wind nor sunlight came, and no sound was heard, and twilight lasted all day long! All round him were trees with straight, tall grey trunks, and behind and beyond them yet other trees—trees everywhere that stood motionless like pillars of stone supporting the dim green roof of foliage far above. It was like a vast gloomy prison in which he had been shut, and he longed to make his escape to where he could see the rising sun and feel the fanning wind on his cheeks. He looked round at the others; they were all stretched on the ground still in a deep sleep, and it frightened him a little to look at their great, broad, dark faces framed in masses of black hair. He felt that he hated them, for they had treated him badly: the children had taken his clothes, compelling him to go naked, and had beaten and bruised him, and he had not been pitied and helped by their elders. By-and-by, very quietly and cautiously he crept away from among them, and made his escape into the gloomy wood.

On one side the forest shadows looked less dark than on the other, and on that side he went, for it was the side on which the sun rose, and the direction he had been travelling when he first met with the savages. On and on he went, over the thick bed of dark decaying leaves, which made no rustling sound, looking like a little white ghost of a boy in that great gloomy wood. But he came to no open place, nor did he find anything to eat when hunger pressed him; for there were no sweet roots and berries there, nor any plant that he had ever seen before. It was all strange and gloomy, and very silent. Not a leaf trembled; for if one had trembled near him he would have heard it whisper in that profound stillness that made him hold his breath to listen. But sometimes at long intervals the silence would be broken by a sound that made him start and stand still and wonder what had caused it. For the rare sounds in the forest were unlike any sounds he had heard before. Three or four times during the day a burst of loud, hollow, confused laughter sounded high up among the trees; but he saw nothing, although most likely the creature that had laughed saw him plainly enough from its hiding-place in the deep shadows as it ran up the trunks of the trees.

At length he came to a river about thirty or forty yards wide; and this was the same river that he had bathed in many leagues further down in the open valley. It is called by the savages Co-viota-co-chamanga, which means that it runs partly in the dark and partly in the light. Here it was in the dark.

D

The trees grew thick and tall on its banks, and their wide branches met and intermingled above its waters that flowed on without a ripple, black to the eye as a river of ink. How strange it seemed when, holding on to a twig, he bent over and saw himself reflected —a white, naked child with a scared face—in that black mirror! Overcome by thirst, he ventured to creep down and dip his hand in the stream, and was astonished to see that the black water looked as clear as crystal in his hollow hand. After quenching his thirst he went on, following the river now, for it had made him turn aside; but after walking for an hour or more he came to a great tree that had fallen across the stream, and climbing on to the slippery trunk, he crept cautiously over and then went gladly on in the old direction.

Now, after he had crossed the river and walked a long distance, he came to a more open part; but though it was nice to feel the sunshine on him again, the underwood and grass and creepers trailing over the ground made it difficult and tiring to walk, and in this place a curious thing happened. Picking his way through the tangled herbage, an animal his footsteps had startled scuttled away in great fear, and as it went he caught a glimpse of it. It was a kind of weasel, but very large—larger than a big tom-cat, and all over as black as the blackest cat. Looking down he discovered that this strange animal had been feasting on eggs. The eggs were nearly as large as fowls', of a deep green colour, with polished shells. There had been about a dozen in the nest, which was only a small hollow in the ground lined with dry grass, but most of them had been broken, and the contents devoured by the weasel. Only two remained entire, and these he took, and tempted by his hunger, soon broke the shells at the small end and sucked them clean. They were raw, but never had eggs, boiled, fried, or poached, tasted so nice before! He had just finished his meal, and was wishing that a third egg had remained in the ruined nest, when a slight sound like the buzzing of an insect made him look round, and there, within a few feet of him, was the big black weasel once more, looking strangely bold and savage-tempered. It kept staring fixedly at Martin out of its small, wicked, beady black eyes, and snarling so as to show its white sharp teeth; and very white they looked by contrast with the black lips, and nose, and hair. Martin stared back at it, but it kept moving and coming nearer, now sitting straight up, then dropping its fore-feet and gathering its legs in a bunch as if about to spring, and finally stretching itself straight out towards him again, its round flat head and long smooth body making it look like a great black snake crawling towards him. And all the time it kept on snarling and clicking its sharp teeth and uttering its low, buzzing growl. Martin grew more and more afraid; it looked so strong and angry, so unspeakably fierce. The creature looked as if he was speaking to Martin, saying something very easy to understand, and very dreadful to hear. This is what it seemed to be saying:

"Ha, you came on me unawares, and startled me

away from the nest I found! You have eaten the last two eggs; and I found them, and they were mine! Must I go hungry for you—starveling, robber! A miserable little boy alone and lost in the forest, naked, all scratched and bleeding with thorns, with no courage in his heart, no strength in his hands! Look at me! I am not weak, but strong and black and fierce; I live here—this is my home; I fear nothing; I am like a serpent, and like brass and tempered steel—nothing can bruise or break me: my teeth are like fine daggers; when I strike them into the flesh of any creature I never loose my hold till I have sucked out all the blood in his heart. But you, weak little wretch, I hate you! I thirst for your blood for stealing my food from me! What can you do to save yourself? Down, down on the ground, chicken heart, where I can get hold of you! You shall pay me for the eggs with your life! I shall hold you fast by the throat, and drink and drink until I see your glassy eyes close, and your cheeks turn whiter than ashes, and I feel your heart flutter like a leaf in your bosom! Down, down!"

It was terrible to watch him and seem to hear such words. He was nearer now—scarcely a yard away, still with his beady glaring eyes fixed on Martin's face: and Martin was powerless to fly from him—powerless even to stir a step or to lift a hand. His heart jumped so that it choked him, his hair stood up on his head, and he trembled so that he was ready to fall. And at last, when about to fall to the ground, in the extremity of his terror, he uttered a great scream of despair; and the sudden scream so startled the weasel, that he jumped up and scuttled away as fast as he could through the creepers and bushes, making a great rustling over the dead leaves and twigs; and Martin, recovering his strength, listened to that retreating sound as it passed away into the deep shadows, until it ceased altogether.

CHAPTER VIII

HIS escape from the horrible black animal made Martin quite happy, in spite of hunger and fatigue, and he pushed on as bravely as ever. But it was slow going and very difficult, even painful in places, on account of the rough thorny undergrowth, where he had to push and crawl through the close bushes, and tread on ground littered with the old dead prickly leaves and dead thorny twigs. After going on for about an hour in this way, he came to a stream, a branch of the river he had left, and much shallower, so that he could easily cross from side to side, and he could also see the bright pebbles under the clear swift current. The stream appeared to run from the east, the way he wished to travel towards the hills, so that he could keep by it, which he was glad enough to do, as it was nice to get a drink of water whenever he felt thirsty, and to refresh his tired and sore little feet in the stream.

Following this water he came before very long to a place in the forest where there was little or no underwood, but only low trees and bushes scattered about, and all the ground moist and very green and fresh like a water-meadow. It was indeed pleasant

54

to feel his feet on the soft carpet of grass, and stooping, he put his hands down on it, and finally lying down he rolled on it so as to have the nice sensation of the warm soft grass all over his body. So agreeable was it lying and rolling about in that open green place with the sweet sunshine on him, that he felt no inclination to get up and travel on. It was so sweet to rest after all his strivings and sufferings in that great dark forest! So sweet was it that he pretty soon fell asleep, and no doubt slept a long time, for when he woke, the sun, which had been over his head, was now far down in the west. It was very still, and the air warm and fragrant at that hour, with the sun shining through the higher branches of the trees on the green turf where he was lying. How green it was—the grass, the trees, every tiny blade and every leaf was like a piece of emerald-green glass with the sun shining through it! So wonderful did it seem to him—the intense greenness, the brilliant sunbeams that shone into his eyes, and seemed to fill him with brightness, and the stillness of the forest, that he sat up and stared about him. What did it mean—that brightness and stillness?

Then at a little distance away, he caught sight of something on a tree of a shining golden-yellow colour. Jumping up he ran to the tree, and found that it was half overgrown with a very beautiful climbing plant, with leaves divided like the fingers of a hand, and large flowers and fruit, both green and ripe. The ripe fruit was as big as a duck's egg, and the same shape, and of a shining yellow colour. Reaching up his hand he began to feel the smooth lovely fruit, when, being very ripe, it came off its stem into his hand. It smelt very nice, and then, in his hunger, he bit through the smooth rind with his teeth, and it tasted as nice as it looked. He quickly ate it, and then pulled another and ate that, and then another, and still others, until he could eat no more. He had not had so delicious a meal for many a long day.

Not until he had eaten his fill did Martin begin to look closely at the flowers on the plant. It was the passion-flower, and he had never seen it before, and now that he looked well at it he thought it the loveliest and strangest flower he had ever beheld; not brilliant and shining, jewel-like, in the sun, like the scarlet verbena of the plains, or some yellow flower, but pale and misty, the petals being of a dim greenish cream-colour, with a large blue circle in the centre; and the blue, too, was misty like the blue haze in the distance on a summer day. To see and admire it better he reached out his hand and tried to pluck one of the flowers; then in an instant he dropped his hand, as if he had been pricked by a thorn. But there was no thorn and nothing to hurt him; he dropped his hand only because he felt that he had hurt the flower. Moving a step back he stared at it, and the flower seemed like a thing alive that looked back at him, and asked him why he had hurt it.

"O, poor flower!" said Martin, and, coming closer he touched it gently with his finger-tips; and then, standing on tiptoe, he touched its petals with his lips, just as his mother had often and often kissed his little hand when he had bruised it or pricked it with a thorn.

Then, while still standing by the plant, on bringing his eyes down to the ground he spied a great snake lying coiled up on a bed of moss on the sunny side of the same tree where the plant was growing. He remembered the dear little snake he had once made a friend of, and he did not feel afraid, for he thought that all snakes must be friendly towards him, although this was a very big one, thicker than his arm and of a different colour. It was a pale olive-green, like the half-dry moss it was lying on, with a pattern of black and brown mottling along its back. It was lying coiled round and round, with its flat arrow-shaped head resting on its coils, and its round bright eyes fixed on Martin's face. The sun shining on its eyes made them glint like polished jewels or pieces of glass, and when Martin moved nearer and stood still, or when he drew back and went to this side or that, those brilliant glinting eyes were still on his face, and it began to trouble him, until at last he covered his face with his hands. Then he opened his fingers enough to peep through them, and still those glittering eyes were fixed on him.

Martin wondered if the snake was vexed with him for coming there, and why it watched him so steadily with those shining eyes. "Will you please look some other way?" he said at last, but the snake would not, and so he turned from it, and then it seemed to him that everything was alive and watching him in the same intent way—the passion-flowers, the green leaves, the grass, the trees, the wide sky, the great shining sun. He listened, and there was no sound in the wood, not even the hum of a fly or wild bee, and it was so still that not a leaf moved. Finally he moved away from that spot, but treading very softly, and holding his breath to listen, for it seemed to him that the forest had something to tell him, and that if he listened he would hear the leaves speaking to him. And by-and-by he did hear a sound: it came from a spot about a hundred yards away, and was like the sound of a person crying. Then came low sobs which rose and fell and then ceased, and after a silent interval began again. Perhaps it was a child, lost there in the forest like himself. Going softly to the spot he discovered that the sobbing sounds came from the other side of a low tree with widespread branches, a kind of acacia with thin loose foliage, but he could not see through it, and so he went round the tree to look, and startled a dove which flew off with a loud clatter of its wings.

When the dove had flown away it was again very silent. What was he to do? He was too tired now to walk much farther, and the sun was getting low, so that all the ground was in shadow. He went on a little way looking for some nice shelter where he could pass the night, but could not find one. At length, when the sun had set and the dark was coming, he came upon an old half-dead tree, where there was a hollow at the roots, lined with half-dry moss, very soft to his foot, and it seemed a nice place to sleep in. But he had no choice, for he was afraid of going further in the dark among the trees; and so, creeping into the hollow among the old roots, he curled himself up as comfortably as he could, and soon began to get very drowsy, in spite of having no covering to keep him warm. But although very tired and sleepy, he did not go quite to sleep, for he had never been all alone in a wood by night before, and it was different from the open plain where he could see all round, even at night, and where he had feared nothing. Here the trees looked strange and made strange black shadows, and he thought that the strange people of the wood were perhaps now roaming about and would find him there. He did not want them to find him fast asleep; it was better to be awake, so that when they came he could jump up and run away and hide himself from them. Once or twice a slight rustling sound made him start and think that at last someone was coming to him, stealing softly so as to catch him unawares, but he could see nothing moving, and when he held his breath to listen there was no sound.

Then all at once, just when he had almost dropped off, a great cry sounded at a distance, and made him start up wide awake again. "O look! look! look!" cried the voice in a tone so deep and strange and powerful that no one could have heard it without terror, for it seemed to be uttered by some forest monster twenty times bigger than an ordinary man. In a moment an answer came from another part of the wood. "What's that?" cried the answering voice; and then another voice cried, and then others far and near, all shouting "What's that?" and for only answer the first voice shouted once more, "O look! look! look!"

Poor Martin, trembling with fright, crouched lower down in his mossy bed, thinking that the awful people of the forest must have seen him, and would be upon him in a few moments. But though he stared with wide-open eyes into the gloom he could see nothing but the trees, standing silent and motionless and no sound of approaching footsteps could he hear.

After that it was silent again for a while, and he began to hope that they had given up looking for him; when suddenly, close by, sounded a loud startling "Who's that?" and he gave himself up for lost. For he was too terrified to jump up and run away, as he had thought to do: he could only lie still, his teeth chattering, his hair standing up on his head. "Who's that?" exclaimed the terrible voice once more, and then he saw a big black shape drop down from the tree above and settle on a dead branch a few feet above his hiding-place. It was a bird— a great owl, for now he could see it, sharply outlined against the clear starry sky; and the bird had seen and was peering curiously at him. And now all his fear was gone, for he could not be afraid of an owl; he had been accustomed to see owls all his life, only they were small, and this owl of the forest was as big as an eagle, and had a round head and ears like a cat, and great cat-like eyes that shone in the dark.

The owl kept staring at Martin for some time, swaying his body this way and that, and lowering then raising his head so as to get a better view. And Martin, on his side, stared back at the owl, and at last he exclaimed, "O what a great big owl you are! Please say *Who's that?* again."

But before the owl said anything Martin was fast asleep in his mossy bed.

CHAPTER IX

WHETHER or not the great owl went on shouting *O look! look! look!* and asking *What's that?* and *Who's that?* all night, Martin did not know. He was fast asleep until the morning sun shone on his face and woke him, and as he had no clothes and shoes to put on he was soon up and out. First he took a drink of water, then, feeling very hungry he went back to the place where he had found the ripe fruit and made a very good breakfast. After that he set out once more through the wood towards sunrise, still following the stream. Before long the wood became still more open, and at last to his great joy he found that he had got clear of it, and was once more on the open plain. And now the hills were once more in sight—those great blue hills where he wished to be, looking nearer and larger than before, but they still looked blue like great banks of cloud and were a long distance away. But he was determined to get to them, to climb up their steep sides, and by-and-by when he found the stream bent away to the south, he left it so as to go on straight as he could to the hills. Away from the water-side the ground was higher, and very flat and covered with dry yellow grass. Over this yellow plain he walked for hours, resting at times, but finding no water and no sweet roots to quench his thirst, until he was too tired to walk any further, and so he sat down on the dry grass under that wide blue sky. There was not a cloud on it—nothing but the great globe of the sun above him; and there was no wind and no motion in the yellow grass-blades, and no sight or sound of any living creature.

Martin lying on his back gazed up at the blue sky, keeping his eyes from the sun, which was too bright for them, and after a time he did see something moving—a small black spot no bigger than a fly moving in a circle. But he knew it was something big, but at so great a height from the earth as to look like a fly. And then he caught sight of a second black speck, then another and another, until he could make out a dozen or twenty, or more, all moving in wide circles at that vast height.

Martin thought they must be the black people of the sky; he wondered why they were black and not white, like white birds, or blue and of other brilliant colours, like the people of the Mirage.

Now it was impossible for Martin to lie like that, following those small black spots on the hot blue sky as they wheeled round and round continuously, without giving his eyes a little rest by shutting them at intervals. By-and-by he kept them shut a little too long; he fell asleep, and when he woke he didn't wake fully in a moment; he remained lying motionless just as before, with eyes still closed, but the lids just raised enough to enable him to see about him.

And the sight that met his eyes was very curious. He was no longer alone in that solitary place. There were people all round him, dozens and scores of little black men about two feet in height, of a very singular appearance. They had bald heads and thin hatchet faces, wrinkled and warty, and long noses; and they all wore black silk clothes — coat, waistcoat and knickerbockers, but without shoes and stockings; their thin black legs and feet were bare; nor did they have anything on their bald heads. They were gathered round Martin in a circle, but a very wide circle quite twenty to thirty feet away from him, and some were walking about, others standing alone or in groups, talking together, and all looking at Martin. Only one who appeared to be the most important person of the company kept inside the circle, and whenever one or more of the others came forward a few steps he held up his hand and begged them to go back a little.

"We must not be in a hurry," he said. "We must wait."

"Wait for what?" asked one.

"For what may happen," said the important one. "I must ask you again to leave it to me to decide when it is time to begin." Then he strutted up and down in the open space, turning now towards his fellows and again to Martin, moving his head about to get a better sight of his face. Then, putting his hand down between his coat and waistcoat he drew out a knife with a long shining blade, and holding it from him looked attentively at it. By-and-by he breathed gently on the bright blade, then pulling out a black silk pocket-handkerchief wiped off the stain of his breath, and turning the blade about made it glitter in the sun. Then he put it back under his coat and resumed his walk up and down.

"We are getting very hungry," said one of the others at length.

"Very hungry indeed!" cried another. "Some of us have not tasted food these three days."

"It certainly does seem hard," said yet another, "to see our dinner before us and not be allowed to touch it."

"Not so fast, my friends, I beg," exclaimed the man with the knife. "I have already explained the case, and I do think you are a little unfair in pressing me as you do."

Thus rebuked they consulted together, then one of them spoke. "If, sir, you consider us unfair, or that we have not full confidence in you, would it not be as well to get some other person to take your place?"

"Yes, I am ready to do that," returned the important one promptly; and here, drawing forth the knife once more, he held it out towards them. But instead of coming forward to take it they all recoiled some steps, showing considerable alarm. And then they all began protesting that they were not complaining of him, that they were satisfied with their choice, and could not have put the matter in abler hands.

"I am pleased at your good opinion," said the

E

important one. "I may tell you that I am no chicken. I first saw the light in September 1739, and, as you know, we are now within seven months and thirteen days of the end of the first decade of the second half of the nineteenth century. You may infer from this that I have had a pretty extensive experience, and I promise you that when I come to cut the body up you will not be able to say that I have made an unfair distribution, or that anyone has been left without his portion."

All murmured approval, and then one of the company asked if he would be allowed to bespeak the liver for his share.

"No, sir, certainly not," replied the other. "Such matters must be left to my discretion entirely, and I must also remind you that there is such a thing as the *carver's privilege*, and it is possible that in this instance he may think fit to retain the liver for his own consumption."

After thus asserting himself he began to examine the blade of his knife which he still held in his hand, and to breathe gently on it, and wipe it with his handkerchief to make it shine brighter in the sun. Finally, raising his arm, he flourished it and then made two or three stabs and lunges in the air, then walking on tiptoe he advanced to Martin lying so still on the yellow grass in the midst of that black-robed company, the hot sun shining on his naked white body.

The others all immediately pressed forward, craning their necks and looking highly excited: they were expecting great things; but when the man with the knife had got quite close to Martin he was seized with fear and made two or three long jumps back to where the others were; and then, recovering from his alarm, he quietly put back the knife under his coat.

"We really thought you were going to begin," said one of the crowd.

"Oh no; no indeed; not just yet," said the other.

"It is very disappointing," remarked one.

The man with the knife turned on him and replied with dignity, "I am really surprised at such a remark after all I have said on the subject. I do wish you would consider the circumstances of the case. They are peculiar, for this person—this Martin— is not an ordinary person. We have been keeping our eyes on him for some time past, and have witnessed some remarkable actions on his part, to put it mildly. Let us keep in mind the boldness, the resource, the dangerous violence he has displayed on so many occasions since he took to his present vagabond way of life."

"It appears to me," said one of the others, "that if Martin is dead we need not concern ourselves about his character and desperate deeds in the past."

"*If* he is dead!" exclaimed the other sharply. "That is the very point,—*is* he dead? Can you confidently say that he is not in a sound sleep, or in a dead faint, or shamming and ready at the first touch of the knife to leap up and seize his assailant

—I mean his carver—by the throat and perhaps murder him as he once murdered a spoonbill?"

"That would be very dreadful," said one.

"But surely," said another, "there are means of telling whether a person is dead or not? One simple and effectual method which I have heard, is to place a hand over the heart to feel if it still beats."

"Yes, I know, I have also heard of that plan. Very simple, as you say; but who is to try it? I invite the person who makes the suggestion to put it in practice."

"With pleasure," said the other, coming forward with a tripping gait and an air of not being in the least afraid. But on coming near the supposed corpse he paused to look round at the others, then pulling out his black silk handkerchief he wiped his black wrinkled forehead and bald head. "Whew!" he exclaimed, "it's very hot to-day."

"I don't find it so," said the man with the knife. "It is sometimes a matter of nerves."

It was not a very nice remark, but it had the effect of bracing the other up, and moving forward a little more he began anxiously scrutinising Martin's face. The others now began to press forward, but were warned by the man with the knife not to come too near. Then the bold person who had undertaken to feel Martin's heart doubled back the silk sleeve of his coat, and after some further preparation extended his arm and made two or three preliminary passes with his trembling hand at a distance of a foot or so from the breast of the corpse. Then he approached it a little nearer, but before it came to the touching point a sudden fear made him start back.

"What is it? What did you see?" cried the others.

"I'm not sure there wasn't a twitch of the eyelid," he replied.

"Never mind the eyelid—feel his heart," said one.

"That's all very well," he returned, "but how would you like it yourself? Will *you* come and do it?"

"No, no!" they all cried. "You have undertaken this, and must go through with it."

Thus encouraged, he once more turned to the corpse, and again anxiously began to examine the face. Now Martin had been watching them through the slits of his not quite closed eyes all the time, and listening to their talk. Being hungry himself he could not help feeling for them, and not thinking that it would hurt him to be cut up in pieces and devoured, he had begun to wish that they would really begin on him. He was both amused and annoyed at their nervousness, and at last opening wide his eyes very suddenly he cried, "Feel my heart!"

It was as if a gun had been fired among them; for a moment they were struck still with terror, and then all together turned and fled, going away with three very long hops, and then opening wide their great wings they launched themselves on the air.

For they were not little black men in black silk clothes as it had seemed, but vultures—those great, high - soaring, black - plumaged birds which he had watched circling in the sky, looking no bigger than bees or flies at that vast distance above the earth.

And when he was watching them they were watching him, and after he had fallen asleep they continued moving round and round in the sky for hours, and seeing him lying so still on the plain they at last imagined that he was dead, and one by one they closed or half-closed their wings and dropped, gliding downwards, growing larger in appearance as they neared the ground, until the small black spots no bigger than flies were seen to be great black birds as big as turkeys.

But you see Martin was not dead after all, and so they had to go away without their dinner.

CHAPTER X

A TROOP OF WILD HORSES

IT seemed so lonely to Martin when the vultures had gone up out of sight in the sky, so silent and solitary on that immense level plain, that he could not help wishing them back for the sake of company. They were an amusing people when they were walking round him, conversing together, and trying without coming too near to discover whether he was dead or only sleeping.

All that day it was just as lonely, for though he went on as far as he could before night, he was still on that great level plain of dry yellow grass which appeared to have no end, and the blue hills looked no nearer than when he had started in the morning. He was hungry and thirsty that evening, and very cold too when he nestled down on the ground with nothing to cover him but the little heap of dry grass he had gathered for his bed.

It was better next day, for after walking two or three hours he came to the end of that yellow plain to higher ground, where the earth was sandy and barren, with a few scattered bushes growing on it —dark, prickly bushes like butcher's broom. When he got to the highest part of this barren ground he saw a green valley beyond, stretching away as far

71

as he could see on either hand. But it was nice to see a green place again, and going down into the valley he managed to find some sweet roots to stay his hunger and thirst; then, after a rest, he went on again, and when he got to the top of the high ground beyond the valley, he saw another valley before him, just like the one he had left behind. Again he rested in that green place, and then slowly went up the high land beyond, where it was barren and sandy with the dark stiff prickly bushes growing here and there, and when he got to the top he looked down, and behold! there was yet another green valley stretching away to the right and left as far as he could see.

Would they never end—these high barren ridges and the long green valleys between!

When he toiled slowly up out of this last green resting-place it was growing late in the day, and he was very tired. Then he came to the top of another ridge like the others, only higher and more barren, and when he could see the country beyond, lo! another valley, greener and broader than those he had left behind, and a river flowing in it, looking like a band of silver lying along the green earth— a river too broad for him to cross, stretching away north and south as far as he could see. How then should he ever be able to get to the hills, still far, far away beyond that water?

Martin stared at the scene before him for some time; then, feeling very tired and weak, he sat down on the sandy ground beside a scanty dark bush.

Tears came to his eyes: he felt them running down his cheeks; and all at once he remembered how long before when his wandering began, he had dropped a tear, and a small dusty beetle had refreshed himself by drinking it. He bent down and let a tear drop, and watched it as it sank into the ground, but no small beetle came out to drink it, and he felt more lonely and miserable than ever. He began to think of all the queer creatures and people he had met in the desert, and to wish for them. Some of them had not been very kind to him, but he did not remember that now, it was so sad to be quite alone in the world without even a small beetle to visit him. He remembered the beautiful people of the Mirage and the black people of the sky; and the ostrich, and old Jacob, and the savages, and the serpent, and the black weasel in the forest. He stood up and stared all round to see if anything was coming, but he could see nothing and hear nothing.

By-and-by, in that deep silence, there was a sound; it seemed to come from a great distance, it was so faint. Then it grew louder and nearer; and far away he saw a little cloud of dust, and then, even through the dust, dark forms coming swiftly towards him. The sound he heard was like a long halloo, a cry like the cry of a man, but wild and shrill, like a bird's cry; and whenever that cry was uttered, it was followed by a strange confused noise as of the neighing of many horses. They were, in truth, horses that were coming swiftly towards him—a herd of sixty or seventy wild horses. He could see and hear them only too plainly now, looking very terrible in their strength and speed, and the flowing black manes that covered them like a black cloud, as they came thundering on, intending perhaps to sweep over him and trample him to death with their iron-hard hoofs.

All at once, when they were within fifty yards of Martin, the long, shrill, wild cry went up again, and the horses swerved to one side, and went sweeping round him in a wide circle. Then, as they galloped by, he caught sight of the strangest-looking being he had ever seen, a man, on the back of one of the horses; naked and hairy, he looked like a baboon as he crouched, doubled up, gripping the shoulders and neck of the horse with his knees, clinging with his hands to the mane, and craning his neck like a flying bird. It was this strange rider who had uttered the long piercing man-and-bird-like cries; and now changing his voice to a whinnying sound the horses came to a stop, and gathering together in a crowd they stood tossing their manes and staring at Martin with their wild, startled eyes.

In another moment the wild rider came bounding out from among them, and moving now erect, now on all fours, came sidling up to Martin, flinging his arms and legs about, wagging his head, grimacing and uttering whinnying and other curious noises. Never had Martin looked upon so strange a man! He was long and lean so that you could have counted his ribs, and he was stark naked, except for the hair of his head and face, which half covered him. His skin was of a yellowish brown colour, and the hair the colour of old dead grass; and it was coarse and tangled, falling over his shoulders and back and covering his forehead like a thatch, his big brown nose standing out beneath it like a beak. The face was covered with the beard, which was tangled too, and grew down to his waist. After staring at Martin for some time with his big yellow, goat-like eyes, he pranced up to him and began to sniff round him, then touched him with his nose on his face, arms, and shoulders.

"Who are you?" said Martin in astonishment.

For only answer the other squealed and whinnied, grimacing and kicking his legs up at the same time. Then the horses advanced to them, and gathering round in a close crowd began touching Martin with their noses. He liked it—the softness of their sensitive skins, which were like velvet, and putting up his hands he began to stroke their noses. Then one by one, after smelling him, and being touched by his hand, they turned away, and going down into the valley were soon scattered about, most of them grazing, some rolling, others lying stretched out on the grass as if to sleep; while the young foals in the troop, leaving their dams, began playing about and challenging one another to run a race.

Martin, following and watching them, almost wished that he too could go on four legs to join them in their games. He trusted those wild horses, but he was still puzzled by that strange man, who had also left him now and was going quietly round on all fours, smelling at the grass. By-and-by he found something to his liking in a small patch of tender green clover, which he began nosing and tearing it up with his teeth, then turning his head round he stared back at Martin, his jaws working vigorously all the time, the stems and leaves of the clover he was eating sticking out from his mouth and hanging about his beard. All at once he jumped up, and flying back at Martin, snatched him up from the ground, carried him to the clover patch, and set him upon it, face down, on all fours; then when Martin sat up he grasped him by the head and forced it down until his nose was on the grass so as to make him smell it and know that it was good. But smell it he would not, and finally the other seized him roughly again and, opening his mouth, forced a bunch of grass into it.

"It's grass, and I sha'n't eat it!" screamed Martin, crying with anger at being so treated, and spewing the green stuff out of his mouth.

Then the man released him, and, withdrawing a space of two or three yards, sat down on his haunches, and, planting his bony elbows on his knees, thrust his great brown fingers in his tangled hair, and stared at Martin with his big yellow goat's eyes for a long time.

Suddenly a wild excited look came into his eyes, and, leaping up with a shrill cry, which caused all the horses to look round at him, he once more snatched Martin up, and holding him firmly gripped to his ribby side by his arm, bounded off to where a mare was standing giving suck to her young foal. With a vigorous kick he sent the foal away, and forced

Martin to take its place, and, to make it easier for
him, pressed the teat into his mouth. Martin was
not accustomed to feed in that way, and he not only
refused to suck, but continued to cry with indigna-
tion at such treatment, and to struggle with all his
little might to free himself. His striving was all in
vain; and by-and-by the man, seeing that he would
not suck, had a fresh idea, and, gripping Martin
more firmly than ever, with one hand forced and held
his mouth open, and with the other drew a stream
of milk into it. After choking and spluttering and
crying more than ever for a while, Martin began to
grow quiet, and to swallow the milk with some
satisfaction, for he was very hungry and thirsty,
and it tasted very good. By-and-by, when no more
milk could be drawn from the teats, he was taken to
a second mare, from which the foal was kicked away
with as little ceremony as the first one, and then he
had as much more milk as he wanted, and began to
like being fed in this amusing way.

Of what happened after that Martin did not know
much, except that the man seemed very happy after
feeding him. He set Martin on the back of a horse,
then jumped and danced round him, making funny
chuckling noises, after which he rolled horse-like on
the grass, his arms and legs up in the air, and finally,
pulling Martin down, he made him roll too.

But the little fellow was too tired to keep his eyes
any longer open, and when he next opened them it
was morning, and he found himself lying wedged
in between a mare and her young foal lying side by

side close together. There too was the wild man, coiled up like a sleeping dog, his head pillowed on the foal's neck, and the hair of his great shaggy beard thrown like a blanket over Martin.

He very soon grew accustomed to the new strange manner of life, and even liked it. Those big, noble-looking wild horses, with their shining coats, brown and bay and black and sorrel and chestnut, and their black manes and tails that swept the grass when they moved, were so friendly to him that he could not help loving them. As he went about among them when they grazed, every horse he approached would raise his head and touch his face and arms with his nose. "O you dear horse!" Martin would exclaim, rubbing the warm, velvet-soft, sensitive nose with his hand.

He soon discovered that they were just as fond of play as he was, and that he too was to take part in their games. Having fed as long as they wanted that morning, they all at once began to gather together, coming at a gallop, neighing shrilly; then the wild man, catching Martin up, leaped upon the back of one of the horses, and away went the whole troop at a furious pace to the great open dry plain, where Martin had met with them on the previous day. Now it was very terrifying for him at first to be in the midst of that flying crowd, as the animals went tearing over the plain, which seemed to shake beneath their thundering hoofs, while their human leader cheered them on with his shrill, repeated cries. But in a little while he too caught the excitement, and, losing all his fear, was as wildly happy as the others, crying out at the top of his voice in imitation of the wild man.

After an hour's run they returned to the valley, and then Martin, without being compelled to do so, rolled about on the grass, and went after the young foals when they came out to challenge one another to a game. He tried to do as they did, prancing and throwing up his heels and snorting, but when they ran from him they soon left him hopelessly behind. Meanwhile the wild man kept watch over him, feeding him with mare's milk, and inviting him from time to time to smell and taste the tender grass. Best of all was when they went for another run in the evening, and when Martin was no longer held with a tight grip against the man's side, but was taught or allowed to hold on, clinging with his legs to the man's body and clasping him round the neck with his arms, his fingers tightly holding on to the great shaggy beard.

Three days passed in this way, and if his time had been much longer with the wild horses he would have become one of the troop, and would perhaps have eaten grass too, and forgotten his human speech, or that he was a little boy born to a very different kind of life. But it was not to be, and in the end he was separated from the troop by accident.

At the end of the third day, when the sun was setting, and all the horses were scattered about in the valley, quietly grazing, something disturbed them.

It might have been a sight or sound of some feared object, or perhaps the wind had brought the smell of their enemies and hunters from a great distance to their nostrils. Suddenly they were all in a wild commotion, galloping from all sides toward their leader, and he, picking Martin up, was quickly on a horse, and off they went full speed, but not towards the plain where they were accustomed to go for their runs. Now they fled in the opposite direction down to the river: into it they went, into that wide, deep, dangerous current, leaping from the bank, each horse, as he fell into the water with a tremendous splash, disappearing from sight; but in another moment the head and upper part of the neck was seen to rise above the surface, until the whole lot were in, and appeared to Martin like a troop of horses' heads swimming without bodies over the river. He, clinging to the neck and beard of the wild man, had the upper half of his body out of the cold, rushing water, and in this way they all got safely across and up the opposite bank. No sooner were they out, than, without even pausing to shake the water from their skins, they set off at full speed across the valley towards the distant hills. Now on this side, at a distance of a mile or so from the river, there were vast reed-beds standing on low land, dried to a hard crust by the summer heat, and right into the reeds the horses rushed and struggled to force their way through. The reeds were dead and dry, so tall that they rose high above the horses' heads, and growing so close together that it was hard to struggle through them. Then, when they were in the midst of this difficult place, the dry crust that covered the low ground began to yield to the heavy hoofs, and the horses, sinking to their knees, were thrown down and plunged about in the most desperate way, and in the midst of this confusion Martin was struck and thrown from his place, falling amongst the reeds. Luckily he was not trampled upon, but he was left behind, and then what a dreadful situation was his, when the whole troop had at last succeeded in fighting their way through, and had gone away leaving him in that dark solitary place! He listened until the sound of heavy hoofs and the long cries of the man had died away in the distance; then the silence and darkness terrified him, and he struggled to get out, but the reeds grew so close together that before he had pushed a dozen yards through them he sank down, unable to do more.

The air was hot and close and still down there on the ground, but by leaning his head back, and staring straight up he could see the pale night sky sprinkled with stars in the openings between the dry leaves and spikes of the reeds. Poor Martin could do nothing but gaze up at the little he could see of the sky in that close, black place, until his neck ached with the strain; but at last, to make him hope, he heard a sound—the now familiar long shrill cry of the wild man. Then, as it came nearer, the sound of tramping hoofs and neighing of the horses was heard, and the cries and hoof-beats grew louder and then fainter in turns, and sounded now on this side, now on that,

F

and he knew that they were looking for him. "I'm here, I'm here," he cried; "oh, dear horses, come and take me away!" But they could not hear him, and at last the sound of their neighing and the wild long cries died away altogether, and Martin was left alone in that black silent place.

CHAPTER XI

THE LADY OF THE HILLS

NO escape was possible for poor little Martin
so long as it was dark, and there he had to
stay all night, but morning brought him
comfort; for now he could see the reed-stems that
hemmed him in all round, and by using his hands
to bend them from him on either side he could push
through them. By-and-by the sunlight touched the
tops of the tall plants, and working his way towards
the side from which the light came he soon made his
escape from that prison, and came into a place where
he could walk without trouble, and could see the earth
and sky again. Further on, in a grassy part of the
valley, he found some sweet roots which greatly
refreshed him, and at last, leaving the valley, he came
out on a high grassy plain, and saw the hills before
him looking very much nearer than he had ever seen
them look before. Up till now they had appeared
like masses of dark blue banked-up cloud resting
on the earth, now he could see that they were indeed
stone—blue stone piled up in huge cliffs and crags
high above the green world; he could see the roughness of the heaped-up rocks, the fissures and crevices
in the sides of the hills, and here and there the patches

of green colour where trees and bushes had taken root. How wonderful it seemed to Martin that evening standing there in the wide green plain, the level sun at his back shining on his naked body, making him look like a statue of a small boy carved in whitest marble or alabaster. Then, to make the sight he gazed on still more enchanting, just as the sun went down the colour of the hills changed from stone-blue to a purple that was like the purple of ripe plums and grapes, only more beautiful and bright. In a few minutes the purple colour faded away and the hills grew shadowy and dark. It was too late in the day, and he was too tired to walk further. He was very hungry and thirsty too, and so when he had found a few small white partridge-berries and had made a poor supper on them, he gathered some dry grass into a little heap, and lying down in it, was soon in a sound sleep.

It was not until the late afternoon next day that Martin at last got to the foot of the hill, or mountain, and looking up he saw it like a great wall of stone above him, with trees and bushes and trailing vines growing out of the crevices and on the narrow ledges of the rock. Going some distance he came to a place where he could ascend, and here he began slowly walking upwards. At first he could hardly contain his delight where everything looked new and strange, and here he found some very beautiful flowers; but as he toiled on he grew more tired and hungry at every step, and then, to make matters worse, his legs began to pain so that he could hardly lift them.

It was a curious pain which he had never felt in his sturdy little legs before in all his wanderings.

Then a cloud came over the sun, and a sharp wind sprang up that made him shiver with cold: then followed a shower of rain; and now Martin, feeling sore and miserable, crept into a cavity beneath a pile of overhanging rocks for shelter. He was out of the rain there, but the wind blew in on him until it made his teeth chatter with cold. He began to think of his mother, and of all the comforts of his lost home—the bread and milk when he was hungry, the warm clothing, and the soft little bed with its snowy white coverlid in which he had slept so sweetly every night.

"O mother, mother!" he cried, but his mother was too far off to hear his piteous cry.

When the shower was over he crept out of his shelter again, and with his little feet already bleeding from the sharp rocks, tried to climb on. In one spot he found some small, creeping, myrtle plants covered with ripe white berries, and although they had a very pungent taste he ate his fill of them, he was so very hungry. Then feeling that he could climb no higher, he began to look round for a dry, sheltered spot to pass the night in. In a little while he came to a great smooth, flat stone that looked like a floor in a room, and was about forty yards wide: nothing grew on it except some small tufts of grey lichen; but on the further side, at the foot of a steep, rocky precipice, there was a thick bed of tall green and yellow ferns, and among the ferns he hoped to find a place to lie down in. Very slowly he limped across the open space, crying with the pain he felt at every step: but when he reached the bed of ferns he all at once saw, sitting among the tall fronds on a stone, a strange-looking woman in a green dress, who was gazing very steadily at him with eyes full of love and compassion. At her side there crouched a big yellow beast, covered all over with black, eye-like spots, with a big round head, and looking just like a cat, but a hundred times larger than the biggest cat he had ever seen. The animal rose up with a low sound like a growl, and glared at Martin with its wide, yellow, fiery eyes, which so terrified him that he dared not move another step until the woman, speaking very gently to him, told him not to fear. She caressed the great beast, making him lie down again; then coming forward and taking Martin by the hand, she drew him up to her knees.

"What is your name, poor little suffering child?" she asked, bending down to him, and speaking softly.

"Martin—what's your's?" he returned, still half sobbing, and rubbing his eyes with his little fists.

"I am called the Lady of the Hills, and I live here alone in the mountain. Tell me, why do you cry, Martin?"

"Because I'm so cold, and—and my legs hurt so, and—and because I want to go back to my mother. She's over there," said he, with another sob, pointing vaguely to the great plain beneath their feet, extending far, far away into the blue distance, where the crimson sun was now setting.

"I will be your mother, and you shall live with me here on the mountain," she said, caressing his little cold hands with hers. "Will you call me mother?"

"You are *not* my mother," he returned warmly. "I don't want to call you mother."

"When I love you so much, dear child?" she pleaded, bending down until her lips were close to his averted face.

"How that great spotted cat stares at me!" he suddenly said. "Do you think it will kill me?"

"No, no, he only wants to play with you. Will you not even look at me, Martin?"

He still resisted her, but her hand felt very warm and comforting—it was such a large, warm, protecting hand. So pleasant did it feel that after a little while he began to move his hand up her beautiful soft, white arm until it touched her hair. For her hair was unbound and loose; it was dark, and finer than the finest spun silk, and fell all over her shoulders, and down her back to the stone she sat on. He let his fingers stray in and out among it; and it felt like the soft, warm down that lines a little bird's nest to his skin. Finally, he touched her neck and allowed his hand to rest there, it was such a soft, warm neck. At length, but reluctantly, for his little rebellious heart was not yet wholly subdued, he raised his eyes to her face. Oh, how beautiful she was! Her love and eager desire to win him had flushed her clear olive skin with rich red colour; out of her sweet red lips, half parted, came her warm breath on his cheek, more fragrant than wild flowers; and her large dark eyes were gazing down into his with such a tenderness in them that Martin, seeing it, felt a strange little shudder pass through him, and scarcely knew whether to think it pleasant or painful. "Dear child, I love you so much," she spoke, "will you not call me mother?"

Dropping his eyes and with trembling lips, feeling a little ashamed at being conquered at last, he whispered "Mother."

She raised him in her arms and pressed him to her bosom, wrapping her hair like a warm mantle round him; and in less than one minute, overcome by fatigue, he fell fast asleep in her arms.

CHAPTER XII

WHEN he awoke Martin found himself lying on a soft downy bed in a dim stone chamber, and feeling silky hair over his cheek and neck and arms, he knew that he was still with his new strange mother, the beautiful Lady of the Mountain. She, seeing him awake, took him up in her arms, and holding him against her bosom, carried him through a long winding stone passage, and out into the bright morning sunlight. There, by a small spring of clearest water that gushed from the rock, she washed his scratched and bruised skin, and rubbed it with sweet-smelling unguents, and gave him food and drink. The great spotted beast sat by them all the time, purring like a cat, and at intervals he tried to entice Martin to leave the woman's lap and play with him. But she would not let him out of her arms: all day she nursed and fondled him as if he had been a helpless babe instead of the sturdy little run-away and adventurer he had proved himself to be. She also made him tell her the story of how he had got lost and of all the wonderful things that had happened to him in his wanderings in the wilderness —the people of the Mirage, and old Jacob and the savages, the great forest, the serpent, the owl, the

89

wild horses and wild man, and the black people of the sky. But it was of the Mirage and the procession of lovely beings about which he spoke most and questioned her.

"Do you think it was all a dream?" he kept asking her, "the Queen and all those people?"

She was vexed at the question, and turning her face away, refused to answer him. For though at all other times, and when he spoke of other things, she was gentle and loving in her manner, the moment he spoke of the Queen of the Mirage and the gifts she had bestowed on him, she became impatient, and rebuked him for saying such foolish things.

At length she spoke and told him that it was a dream, a very very idle dream, a dream that was not worth dreaming; that he must never speak of it again, never think of it, but forget it, just as he had forgotten all other vain silly dreams he had ever had. And having said this much a little sharply, she smiled again and fondled him, and promised that when he next slept he should have a good dream, one worth the dreaming, and worth remembering and talking about.

She held him away from her, seating him on her knees, to look at his face, and said, "For oh, dear little Martin, you are lovely and sweet to look at, and you are mine, my own sweet child, and so long as you live with me on the hills, and love me and call me mother, you shall be happy, and everything you see, sleeping and waking, shall seem strange and beautiful."

It was quite true that he was sweet to look at, very pretty with his rosy-white skin deepening to red on his cheeks; and his hair curling all over his head was of a bright golden chestnut colour; and his eyes were a very bright blue, and looked keen and straight at you just like a bird's eyes, that seem to be thinking of nothing, and yet seeing everything.

After this Martin was eager to go to sleep at once and have the promised dream, but his very eagerness kept him wide awake all day, and even after going to bed in that dim chamber in the heart of the hill, it was a long time before he dropped off. But he did not know that he had fallen asleep: it seemed to him that he was very wide awake, and that he heard a voice speaking in the chamber, and that he started up to listen to it.

"Do you not know that there are things just as strange underground as above it?" said the voice.

Martin could not see the speaker, but he answered quite boldly: "No — there's nothing underground except earth and worms and roots. I've seen it when they've been digging."

"Oh, but there is!" said the voice. "You can see for yourself. All you've got to do is to find a path leading down, and to follow it. There's a path over there just in front of you; you can see the opening from where you are lying."

He looked, and sure enough there *was* an opening, and a dim passage running down through the solid rock. Up he jumped, fired at the prospect of seeing new and wonderful things, and without looking any more to see who had spoken to him, he ran over to it. The passage had a smooth floor of stone, and sloped downward into the earth, and went round and round in an immense spiral; but the circles were so wide that Martin scarcely knew that he was not travelling in a straight line. Have you by chance ever seen a buzzard, or stork, or vulture, or some other great bird, soaring upwards into the sky in wide circles, each circle taking it higher above the earth, until it looked like a mere black speck in the vast blue heavens, and at length disappeared altogether? Just in that way, going round and round in just such wide circles, lightly running all the time, with never a pause to rest, and without feeling in the least tired, Martin went on, only down and down and further down, instead of up and up like the soaring bird, until he was as far under the mountain as ever any buzzard or crane or eagle soared above it.

Thus running he came at last out of the passage to an open room or space so wide that, look which way he would, he could see no end to it. The stone roof of this place was held up by huge stone pillars standing scattered about like groups of great rough-barked trees, many times bigger round than hogsheads. Here and there in the roof, or the stone overhead, were immense black caverns which almost frightened him to gaze up at them, they were so vast and black. And no light of sun or moon came down into that deep part of the earth: the light was from big fires, and they were fires of smithies burning all about him, sending up great flames and clouds of black smoke, which rose and floated upwards through those big black caverns in the roof. Crowds of people were gathered around the smithies, all very busy beating and hammering on anvils like blacksmiths. Never had he seen so many people, nor ever had he seen such busy men as these, rushing about here and there shouting and colliding with one another, bringing and carrying huge loads in baskets on their backs, and altogether the sight of them, and the racket and the smoke and dust, and the blazing fires, was almost too much for Martin; and for a moment or two he was tempted to turn and run back into the passage through which he had come. But the strangeness of it all kept him there, and then he began to look more closely at the people, for these were the little men that live under the earth, and they were unlike anything he had seen on its surface. They were very stout, strong-looking little men, dressed in coarse dark clothes, covered with dust and grime, and they had dark faces, and long hair, and rough, unkempt beards; they had very long arms and big hands, like baboons, and there was not one among them who looked taller than Martin himself. After looking at them he did not feel at all afraid of them; he only wanted very much to know who they were, and what they were doing, and why they were so excited and noisy over their work. So he thrust himself among them, going to the smithies where they were in crowds, and peering curiously at them. Then he began to notice that his coming among them created a great commotion, for no sooner would he appear than all work would be instantly suspended; down would go their baskets and loads of wood, their hammers and implements of all kinds, and they would stare and point at him, all jabbering together, so that the noise was as if a thousand cockatoos and parrots and paroquets were all screaming at once. What it was all about he could not tell, as he could not make out what they said; he could only see, and plainly enough, that his presence astonished and upset them, for as he went about among them they fell back before him, crowding together, and all staring and pointing at him.

But at length he began to make out what they were saying; they were all exclaiming and talking about him. "Look at him! look at him!" they cried. "Who is he? What, Martin—this Martin? Never. No, no, no! Yes, yes, yes! Martin himself—Martin with nothing on! Not a shred—not a thread! Impossible—it cannot be! Nothing so strange has ever happened! *Naked*—do you say that Martin is naked? Oh, dreadful — from the crown of his head to his toes, naked as he was born! No clothes—no clothes— oh no, it can't be Martin. It is, it is!" And so on and on, until Martin could not endure it longer, for he had been naked for days and days, and had ceased to think about it, and in fact did not know that he was naked. And now hearing their remarks, and seeing how they were disturbed, he looked down at himself and saw that it was indeed so—that he had nothing on, and he grew ashamed and frightened, and thought he would run and hide himself from them in some hole in the ground. But there was no place to hide in, for now they had gathered all round him in a vast crowd, so that whichever way he turned there before him they appeared—hundreds and hundreds of dark, excited faces, hundreds of grimy hands all pointing at him. Then, all at once, he caught sight of an old rag of a garment lying on the ground among the ashes and cinders, and he thought he would cover himself with it, and picking it hastily up was just going to put it round him when a great roar of "No!" burst out from the crowd; he was almost deafened with the sound, so that he stood trembling with the old dirty rag of cloth in his hand. Then one of the Little Men came up to him, and snatching the rag from his hand, flung it angrily down upon the floor; then, as if afraid of remaining so near Martin, he backed away into the crowd again.

Just then Martin heard a very low voice close to his ear speaking to him, but when he looked round he could see no person near him. He knew it was the same voice which had spoken to him in the cave where he slept, and had told him to go down into that place underground.

"Do not fear," said the gentle voice to Martin. "Say to the Little Men that you have lost your clothes, and ask them for something to put on."

Then Martin, who had covered his face with his hands to shut out the sight of the angry crowd, took courage, and looking at them, said, half sobbing, "O, Little Men, I've lost my clothes—won't you give me something to put on?"

This speech had a wonderful effect: instantly

there was a mighty rush, all the Little Men hurrying away in all directions, shouting and tumbling over each other in their haste to get away, and by-and-by it looked to Martin as if they were having a great struggle or contest over something. They were all struggling to get possession of a small closed basket, and it was like a game of football with hundreds of persons all playing, all fighting for possession of the ball. At length one of them succeeded in getting hold of the basket and escaping from all the others who opposed him, and running to Martin he threw it down at his feet, and lifting the lid displayed to his sight a bundle of the most beautiful clothes ever seen by child or man. With a glad cry Martin pulled them out, but the next moment a very important-looking Little Man, with a great white beard, sprang forward and snatched them out of his hand.

"No, no," he shouted. "These are not fit for Martin to wear! They will soil!" Saying which, he flung them down on that dusty floor with its litter of cinders and dirt, and began to trample on them as if in a great passion. Then he snatched them up again and shook them, and all could see that they were unsoiled and just as bright and beautiful as before. Then Martin tried to take them from him, but the other would not let him.

"Never shall Martin wear such poor clothes," shouted the old man. "They will not even keep out the wet," and with that he thrust them into a great tub of water, and jumping in began treading them down with his feet. But when he pulled them out again and shook them before their faces, all saw that they were as dry and bright as before.

"Give them to me!" cried Martin, thinking that it was all right now.

"Never shall Martin wear such poor clothes—they will not resist fire," cried the old man, and into the flames he flung them.

Martin now gave up all hopes of possessing them, and was ready to burst into tears at their loss, when out of the fire they were pulled again, and it was seen that the flames had not injured or tarnished them in the least. Once more Martin put out his arms and this time he was allowed to take those beautiful clothes, and then just as he clasped them to him with a cry of delight he woke!

His head was lying on his new mother's arm, and she was awake watching him.

"O, mother, what a nice dream I had! O such pretty clothes—why did I wake so soon?"

She laughed and touched his arms, showing him that they were still clasping that beautiful suit of clothes to his breast — the very clothes of his wonderful dream!

G

CHAPTER XIII

THERE was not in all that land, nor perhaps in all the wide world, a happier little boy than Martin, when after waking from his sleep and dream he dressed himself for the first time in that new suit, and went out from the cave into the morning sunlight. He then felt the comfort of such clothes, for they were softer than the finest, softest down or silk to his skin, and kept him warm when it was cold, and cool when it was hot, and dry when it rained on him, and the earth could not soil them, nor the thorns tear them; and above everything they were the most beautiful clothes ever seen. Their colour was a deep moss-green, or so it looked at a little distance, or when seen in the shade, but in the sunshine it sparkled as if small, shining, many-coloured beads had been sewn in the cloth; only there were no beads; it was only the shining threads that made it sparkle so, like clean sand in the sun. When you looked closely at the cloth, you could see the lovely pattern woven in it—small leaf and flower, the leaves like moss leaves, and the flowers like the pimpernel, but not half so big, and they were yellow and red and blue and violet in colour.

98

But there were many, many things besides the lovely clothes to make him contented and happy. First, the beautiful woman of the hills who loved and cherished him and made him call her by the sweet name of "mother" so many times every day that he well-nigh forgot she was not his real mother. Then there was the great stony hillside on which he now lived for a playground, where he could wander all day among the rocks, overgrown with creepers and strange sweet-smelling flowers he had never seen on the plain below. The birds and butterflies he saw there were different from those he had always seen; so were the snakes which he often found sleepily coiled up on the rocks, and the little swift lizards. Even the water looked strange and more beautiful than the water in the plain, for here it gushed out of the living rock, sparkling like crystal in the sun, and was always cold when he dipped his hands in it even on the hottest days. Perhaps the most wonderful thing was the immense distance he could see, when he looked away from the hillside across the plain and saw the great dark forest where he had been, and the earth stretching far, far away beyond.

Then there was his playmate, the great yellow-spotted cat, who followed him about and was always ready for a frolic, playing in a very curious way. Whenever Martin would prepare to take a running leap, or a swift run down a slope, the animal, stealing quietly up behind, would put out a claw from his big soft foot—a great white claw as big as an owl's beak—and pull him suddenly back. At last Martin would lose his temper, and picking up a stick would turn on his playmate; and away the animal would fly, pretending to be afraid, and going over bushes and big stones with tremendous leaps to disappear from sight on the mountain-side. But very soon he would steal secretly back by some other way to spring upon Martin unawares and roll him over and over on the ground, growling as if angry, and making believe to worry him with his great white teeth, although never really hurting him in the least. He played with Martin just as a cat plays with its kitten when it pretends to punish it.

Whenever Martin began to show the least sign of weariness the Lady of the Hills would call him to her. Then, lying back among the ferns, she would unbind her long silky tresses to let him play with them, for this was always a delight to him. Then she would gather her hair up again and dress it with yellow flowers and glossy dark green leaves to make herself look more lovely than ever. At other times, taking him on her shoulders, she would bound nimbly as a wild goat up the steepest places, springing from crag to crag, and dancing gaily along the narrow ledges of rock, where it made him dizzy to look down. Then when the sun was near setting, when long shadows from rocks and trees began to creep over the mountain, and he had eaten the fruits and honey and other wild delicacies she provided, she would make him lie on her bosom. Playing with her loose hair and listening to her singing as she rocked herself on a stone, he would presently fall asleep.

In the morning on waking he would always find himself lying still clasped to her breast in that great dim cavern; and almost always when he woke he would find her crying. Sometimes on opening his eyes he would find her asleep, but with traces of tears on her face, showing that she had been awake and crying.

One afternoon, seeing him tired of play and hard to amuse, she took him in her arms and carried him right up the side of the mountain, where it grew so steep that even the big cat could not follow them. Finally she brought him out on the extreme summit, and looking round he seemed to see the whole world spread out beneath him. Below, half-way down, there were some wild cattle feeding on the mountain-side, and they looked at that distance no bigger than mice. Looking eastwards he beheld just beyond the plain a vast expanse of blue water extending leagues and leagues away until it faded into the blue sky. He shouted with joy when he saw it, and could not take his eyes from this wonderful world of water.

"Take me there—take me there!" he cried.

She only shook her head and tried to laugh him out of such a wish; but by-and-by when she attempted to carry him back down the mountain he refused to move from the spot; nor would he speak to her nor look up into her pleading face, but kept his eyes fixed on that distant blue ocean which had so enchanted him. For it seemed to Martin the most wonderful thing he had ever beheld.

At length it began to grow cold on the summit;

then with gentle caressing words she made him turn and look to the opposite side of the heavens, where the sun was just setting behind a great mass of clouds—dark purple and crimson, rising into peaks that were like hills of rose-coloured pearl, and all the heavens beyond them a pale primrose-coloured flame. Filled with wonder at all this rich and varied colour he forgot the ocean for a moment, and uttered an exclamation of delight.

"Do you know, dear Martin," said she, "what we should find there, where it all looks so bright and beautiful, if I had wings and could fly with you clinging to my bosom like a little bat clinging to its mother when she flies abroad in the twilight?"

"What?" asked Martin.

"Only dark, dark clouds full of rain and cutting hail and thunder and lightning. That is how it is with the sea, Martin: it makes you love it when you see it at a distance; but oh, it is cruel and treacherous, and when it has once got you in its power then it is more terrible than the thunder and lightning in the cloud. Do you remember, when you first came to me, naked, shivering with cold, with your little bare feet blistered and bleeding from the sharp stones, how I comforted you with my love, and you found it warm and pleasant lying on my breast? The sea will not comfort you in that way; it will clasp you to a cold, cold breast, and kiss you with bitter salt lips, and carry you down where it is always dark, where you will never, never see the blue sky and sunshine and flowers again."

Martin shivered and nestled closer to her; and then while the shadows of evening were gathering round them, she sat rocking herself to and fro on a stone, murmuring many tender, sweet words to him, until the music of her voice and the warmth of her bosom made him sleep.

CHAPTER XIV

THE WONDERS OF THE HILLS

NOW, although Martin had gone very comfortably to sleep in her arms and found it sweet to be watched over so tenderly, he was not the happy little boy he had been before the sight of the distant ocean. And she knew it, and was troubled in her mind, and anxious to do something to make him forget that great blue water. She could do many things, and above all she could show him new and wonderful things in the hills where she wished to keep him always with her. To caress him, to feed and watch over him by day, and hold him in her arms when he slept at night—all that was less to him than the sight of something new and strange; she knew this well, and therefore determined to satisfy his desire and make his life so full that he would always be more than contented with it.

In the morning he went out on the hillside, wandering listlessly among the rocks, and when the big cat found him there and tried to tempt him to a game he refused to play, for he had not yet got over his disappointment, and could think of nothing but the sea. But the cat did not know that anything was the matter with him, and was more determined to play than ever; crouching now here, now there among

the stones and bushes, he would spring out upon
Martin and pull him down with its big paws, and this
so enraged him that picking up a stick he struck
furiously at his tormentor. But the cat was too
quick for him; he dodged the blows, then knocked
the stick out of his hand, and finally Martin, to escape
from him, crept into a crevice in a rock where the cat
could not reach him, and refused to come out even
when the Lady of the Hills came to look for him and
begged him to come to her. When at last, compelled
by hunger, he returned to her, he was silent and
sullen and would not be caressed.

He saw no more of the cat, and when next day
he asked her where it was, she said that it had gone
from them and would return no more—that she had
sent it away because it had vexed him. This made
Martin sulk, and he would have gone away and
hidden himself from her had she not caught him up
in her arms. He struggled to free himself, but could
not, and she then carried him away a long distance
down the mountain-side until they came to a small
dell, green with creepers and bushes, with a deep
carpet of dry moss on the ground, and here she sat
down and began to talk to him.

"The cat was a very beautiful beast with his
spotted hide," she said; "and you liked to play with
him sometimes, but in a little while you will be glad
that he has gone from you."

He asked her why.

"Because though he was fond of you and liked
to follow you about and play with you, he is very

fierce and powerful, and all the other beasts are afraid of him. So long as he was with us they would not come, but now he has gone they will come to you and let you go to them."

"Where are they?" said Martin, his curiosity greatly excited.

"Let us wait here," she said, "and perhaps we shall see one by-and-by."

So they waited and were silent, and as nothing came and nothing happened, Martin sitting on the mossy ground began to feel a strange drowsiness stealing over him. He rubbed his eyes and looked round; he wanted to keep very wide awake and alert, so as not to miss the sight of anything that might come. He was vexed with himself for feeling drowsy, and wondered why it was; then listening to the low continuous hum of the bees, he concluded that it was that low, soft, humming sound that made him sleepy. He began to look at the bees, and saw that they were unlike other wild bees he knew, that they were like humble-bees in shape but much smaller, and were all of a golden-brown colour: they were in scores and hundreds coming and going, and had their home or nest in the rock a few feet above his head. He got up, and climbing from his mother's knee to her shoulder, and standing on it, he looked into the crevice into which the bees were streaming, and saw their nest full of clusters of small. round objects that looked like white berries.

Then he came down and told her what he had seen, and wanted to know all about it, and when she answered that the little round fruit-like objects he had seen were cells full of purple honey that tasted sweet and salt, he wanted her to get him some.

"Not now — not to-day," she replied, "for now you love me and are contented to be with me, and you are my own darling child. When you are naughty, and try to grieve me all you can, and would like to go away and never see me more, you shall taste the purple honey."

He looked up into her face wondering and troubled at her words, and she smiled down so sweetly on his upturned face, looking very beautiful and tender, that it almost made him cry to think how wilful and passionate he had been, and climbing on to her knees he put his little face against her cheek.

Then, while he was still caressing her, light tripping steps were heard over the stony path, and through the bushes came two beautiful wild animals —a doe with her fawn! Martin had often seen the wild deer on the plains, but always at a great distance and running; now that he had them standing before him he could see just what they were like, and of all the four-footed creatures he had ever looked on they were undoubtedly the most lovely. They were of a slim shape, and of a very bright reddish fawn-colour, the young one with dappled sides; and both had large trumpet-like ears, which they held up as if listening, while they gazed fixedly at Martin's face with their large, dark, soft eyes. Enchanted with the sight of them, he slipped down from his mother's lap, and stretched out his arms towards them, and the doe, coming a little nearer, timidly smelt at his hand, then licked it with her long, pink tongue.

In a few minutes the doe and fawn went away and they saw them no more; but they left Martin with a heart filled with happy excitement; and they were but the first of many strange and beautiful wild animals he was now made acquainted with, so that for days he could think of nothing else and wished for nothing better.

But one day when she had taken him a good way up on the hillside, Martin suddenly recognised a huge rocky precipice before him as the one up which she had taken him, and from the top of which he had seen the great blue water. Instantly he demanded to be taken up again, and when she refused, he rebelled against her, and was first passionate and then sullen. Finding that he would not listen to anything she could say, she sat down on a rock and left him to himself. He could not climb up that precipice, and so he rambled away to some distance, thinking to hide himself from her, because he thought her unreasonable and unkind not to allow him to see the blue water once more. But presently he caught sight of a snake lying motionless on a bed of moss at the foot of a rock, with the sun on it, lighting up its polished scales so that they shone like gems or coloured glass. Resting his elbows on the stone and holding his face between his hands he fell to watching the snake, for though it seemed fast asleep in the sun its gem-like eyes were wide open.

All at once he felt his mother's hand on his head: "Martin," she said, "would you like to know what the snake feels when it lies with eyes open in the bright hot sun? Shall I make you feel just how he feels?"

"Yes," said Martin eagerly, forgetting his quarrel with her; then taking him up in her strong arms she walked rapidly away, and brought him to that very spot where he had seen the doe and fawn.

She set him down, and instantly his ears were filled with the murmur of the bees; and in a moment she put her hand in the crevice and pulled out a cluster of white cells, and gave them to Martin. Breaking one of the cells he saw that it was full of thick honey, of a violet colour, and tasting it he found it was like very sweet honey in which a little salt has been mixed. He liked it and he didn't like it; still, it was not the same in all the cells; in some it was scarcely salt at all; and he began to suck the honey of cell after cell, trying to find one that was not salt; and by-and-by he dropped the cluster of cells from his hand, and stooping to pick it up forgot to do so, and laying his head down and stretching himself out on the mossy ground looked up into his mother's face with drowsy, happy eyes. How sweet it seemed, lying there in the sun, with the sun shining right into his eyes, and filling his whole being with its delicious heat! He wished for nothing now—not even for the sight of new wonderful things; he forgot the blue water, the strange, beautiful wild animals, and his only thought, if he had a thought, was that it was very nice to lie there, not sleeping, but feeling the sun in him, and seeing it above him; and seeing all things—the blue sky, the grey rocks and green bushes and moss, and the woman in her green dress and her loose black hair—and hearing, too, the soft, low, continuous murmur of the yellow bees.

For hours he lay there in that drowsy condition, his mother keeping watch over him, and when it passed off, and he got up again, his temper appeared changed: he was more gentle and affectionate with his mother, and obeyed her every wish. And when in his rambles on the hill he found a snake lying in the sun he would steal softly near it and watch it steadily for a long time, half wishing to taste that strange purple honey again, so that he might lie again in the sun, feeling what the snake feels. But there were more wonderful things yet for Martin to see and know in the hills, so that in a little while he ceased to have that desire.

CHAPTER XV

ONE morning when they went up into a wild rocky place very high up on the hillside, a number of big birds were seen coming over the mountain at a great height in the air, travelling in a northerly direction. They were big hawks almost as big as eagles, with very broad rounded wings, and instead of travelling straight like other birds they moved in wide circles, so that they progressed very slowly.

They sat down on a stone to watch the birds, and whenever one flying lower than the others came pretty near them Martin gazed delightedly at it, and wished it would come still nearer so that he might see it better. Then the woman stood up on the stone, and, gazing skywards and throwing up her arms, she uttered a long call, and the birds began to come lower and lower down, still sweeping round in wide circles, and by-and-by one came quite down and pitched on a stone a few yards from them. Then another came and lighted on another stone, then another, and others followed, until they were all round him in scores, sitting on the rocks, great brown birds with black bars on their wings and tails,

III

and buff-coloured breasts with rust-red spots and stripes. It was a wonderful sight, those eagle-like hawks, with their blue hooked beaks and deep-set dark piercing eyes, sitting in numbers on the rocks, and others and still others dropping down from the sky to increase the gathering.

Then the woman sat down by Martin's side, and after a while one of the hawks spread his great wings and rose up into the air to resume his flight. After an interval of a minute or so another rose, then another, but it was an hour before they were all gone.

"O the dear birds — they are all gone!" cried Martin. "Mother, where are they going?"

She told him of a far-away land in the south, from which, when autumn comes, the birds migrate north to a warmer country hundreds of leagues away, and that birds of all kinds were now travelling north, and would be travelling through the sky above them for many days to come.

Martin looked up at the sky, and said he could see no birds now that the buzzards were all gone.

"I can see them," she returned, looking up and glancing about the sky.

"O mother, I wish I could see them!" he cried. "Why can't I see them when you can?"

"Because your eyes are not like mine. Look, can you see this?" and she held up a small stone phial which she took from her bosom.

He took it in his hand and unstopped and smelt at it. "Is it honey? Can I taste it?" he asked.

She laughed. "It is better than honey, but you

can't eat it!" she said. "Do you remember how the honey made you feel like a snake? This would make you see what I see if I put some of it on your eyes."

He begged her to do so, and she consenting poured a little into the palm of her hand. It was thick and white as milk; then taking some on her finger tip, she made him hold his eyes wide open while she rubbed it on the eye-balls. It made his eyes smart, and everything at first looked like a blue mist when he tried to see; then slowly the mist faded away and the air had a new marvellous clearness, and when he looked away over the plain beneath them he shouted for joy, so far could he see and so distinct did distant objects appear. At one point where nothing but the grey haze that obscured the distance had been visible, a herd of wild cattle now appeared, scattered about, some grazing, others lying down ruminating, and in the midst of the herd a very noble-looking, tawny-coloured bull was standing.

"O mother, do you see that bull?" cried Martin in delight.

"Yes, I see him," she returned. "Sometimes he brings his herd to feed on the hillside, and when I see him here another time I shall take you to him, and put you on his back. But look now at the sky, Martin."

He looked up and was astonished to see numbers of great birds flying north, where no birds had appeared before. They were miles high, and invisible to ordinary sight, but he could see them so distinctly, their shape and colours, that all the birds

H

he knew were easily recognised. There were swans, shining white, with black heads and necks, flying in wedge - shaped flocks, and rose - coloured spoonbills, and flamingoes with scarlet wings tipped with black, and ibises, and ducks of different colours, and many other birds, both water and land, appeared, flock after flock, all flying as fast as their wings could bear them towards the north.

He continued watching them until it was past noon, and then he saw fewer and fewer, only very big birds, appearing; and then these were seen less and less until there were none. Then he turned his eyes on the plain and tried to find the herd of wild cattle, but they were no longer visible; it was as he had seen it in the morning with the pale blue haze over all the distant earth. He was told that the power to see all distant things with a vision equal to his mother's was now exhausted, and when he grieved at the loss she comforted him with the promise that it would be renewed at some other time.

Now one day when they were out together Martin was greatly surprised and disturbed at a change in his mother. When he spoke to her she was silent; and by-and-by, drawing a little away, he looked at her with a fear which increased to a kind of terror, so strangely altered did she seem, standing motionless, gazing fixedly with wide-open eyes at the plain beneath them, her whole face white and drawn with a look of rage. He had an impulse to fly from her and hide himself in some hole in the rocks from the sight of that pale, wrathful face, but when he looked round he was afraid to move from her, for the hill itself seemed changed, and now looked black and angry even as she did. The ground he stood on, the grey old stones covered with silvery-white and yellow lichen and pretty flowery, creeping plants, so beautiful to look at in the bright sunlight a few moments ago, now were covered with a dull mist which appeared to be rising from them, making the air around them dark and strange. And the air, too, had become sultry and close, and the sky was growing dark above them. Then suddenly remembering all her love and kindness he flew to her, and clinging to her dress sobbed out, "O mother, mother, what is it?"

She put her hand on him, then drew him up to her side with his feet on the stone she was standing by. "Would you like to see what I see, Martin?" she asked, and taking the phial from her bosom she rubbed the white thick liquid on his eye-balls, and in a little while, when the mistiness passed off, she pointed with her hand and told him to look there.

He looked, and as on the former occasion, all distant things were clearly visible, for although that mist and blackness given off by the hill had wrapped them round so that they seemed to be standing in the midst of a black cloud, yet away on the plain beneath the sun was shining brightly, and all that was there could be seen by him. Where he had once seen a herd of wild cattle he now saw mounted men, to the number of about a dozen, slowly riding towards the hill, and though they were miles away he could see them very distinctly. They were dark, black-bearded men, strangely dressed, some with fawn-coloured cloaks with broad stripes, others in a scarlet uniform, and they wore cone-shaped scarlet caps. Some carried lances, others carbines; and they all wore swords—he could see the steel scabbards shining in the sun. As he watched them they drew rein and some of them got off their horses, and they stood for some time as if talking excitedly, pointing towards the hill and using emphatic gestures.

What were they talking about so excitedly? thought Martin. He wanted to know, and he would have asked her, but when he looked up at her she was still gazing fixedly at them with the same pale face and terrible stern expression, and he could but dimly see her face in that black cloud which had closed around them. He trembled with fear and could only murmur, "Mother! mother!" Then her arm was put round him, and she drew him close against her side, and at that moment—O how terrible it was!—the black cloud and the whole universe was lit up with a sudden flash that seemed to blind and scorch him, and the hill and the world was shaken and seemed to be shattered by an awful thunder crash. It was more than he could endure: he ceased to feel or know anything, and was like one dead, and when he came to himself and opened his eyes he was lying in her lap with her face smiling very tenderly, bending over him.

"Oh, poor little Martin," she said, "what a poor, weak little boy you are to lose your senses at the lightning and thunder! I was angry when I saw them coming to the hill, for they are wicked, cruel men, stained with blood, and I made the storm to drive them away. They are gone, and the storm is over now, and it is late—come, let us go to our cave"; and she took him up and carried him in her arms.

CHAPTER XVI

THE PEOPLE OF THE MIST

WHEN Martin first came to the hills it was at the end of the long, hot, dry summer of that distant land: it was autumn now, and the autumn was like a second summer, only not so hot and dry as the first. But sometimes at this season a wet mist came up from the sea by night and spread over all the country, covering it like a cloud; to a soaring bird looking down from the sky it must have appeared like another sea of a pale or pearly-grey colour, with the hills rising like islands from it. When the sun rose in the morning, if the sky was clear so that it could shine, then the sea-fog would drift and break up and melt away or float up in the form of thin white clouds. Now, whenever this sea-mist was out over the world the Lady of the Hills, without coming out of her chamber, knew of it, and she would prevent Martin from leaving the bed and going out. He loved to be out on the hillside, to watch the sun come up, and she would say to him, "You cannot see the sun because of the mist: and it is cold and wet on the hill; wait until the mist has gone and then you shall go out."

But now a new idea came into her mind. She

had succeeded in making him happy during the last few days; but she wished to do more—she wished to make him fear and hate the sea so that he would never grow discontented with his life on the hills nor wish to leave her. So now, one morning, when the mist was out over the land, she said to Martin when he woke, "Get up and go out on to the hill and see the mist; and when you feel its coldness and taste its salt on your lips, and see how it dims and saddens the earth, you will know better than to wish for that great water it comes from."

So Martin got up and went out on the hill, and it was as she had said: there was no blue sky above, no wide green earth before him: the mist had blotted all out; he could hardly see the rocks and bushes a dozen yards from him; the leaves and flowers were heavy laden with the grey wet; and it felt clammy and cold on his face, and he tasted its salt on his lips. It seemed thickest and darkest when he looked down and lightest when he looked up, and the lightness led him to climb up among the dripping, slippery rocks; and slipping and stumbling he went on and on, the light increasing as he went, until at last to his delight he got above the mist. There was an immense crag there which stood boldly up on the hillside, and on to this he managed to climb, and standing on it he looked down upon that vast moving sea of grey mist that covered the earth, and saw the sun, a large crimson disc, rising from it.

It was a great thing to see, and made him cry out aloud for joy: and then as the sun rose higher into the pure, blue sky the grey mist changed to silvery white, and the white changed in places to shining gold: and it drifted faster and faster away before the sun, and began to break up, and when a cloud of mist swept by the rock on which he stood it beat like a fine rain upon his face, and covered his bright clothes with a grey beady moisture.

Now, looking abroad over the earth, it appeared to Martin that the thousands and tens and hundreds of thousands of fragments of mist had the shapes of men, and were like an innumerable multitude of gigantic men with shining white faces and shining golden hair and long cloud-like robes of a pearly-grey colour, that trailed on the earth as they moved. They were like a vast army covering the whole earth, all with their faces set towards the west, all moving swiftly and smoothly on towards the west. And he saw that every one held his robes to his breast with his left hand, and that in his right hand, raised to the level of his head, he carried a strange object. This object was a shell—a big sea-shell of a golden-yellow colour with curved pink lips; and very soon one of the mist people came near him, and as he passed by the rock he held the shell to Martin's ear, and it sounded in his ear—a low, deep murmur as of waves breaking on a long shingled beach, and Martin knew, though no word was spoken to him, that it was the sound of the sea, and tears of delight came to his eyes, and at the same time his heart was sick and sad with longing for the sea.

Again and again, until the whole vast multitude

of the mist people had gone by, a shell was held to his ear; and when they were all gone, when he had watched them fade like a white cloud over the plain, and float away and disappear in the blue sky, he sat down on the rock and cried with the desire that was in him.

When his mother found him with traces of tears on his cheeks, and he was silent when she spoke to him, and had a strange look in his eyes as if they were gazing at some distant object, she was angrier than ever with the sea, for she knew that the thought of it had returned to him and that it would be harder than ever to keep him.

One morning on waking he found her still asleep, although the traces of tears on her cheeks showed that she had been awake and crying during the night.

"Ah, now I know why she cries every morning," thought Martin; "it is because I must go away and leave her here alone on the hills."

He was out of her arms and dressed in a very few moments, moving very softly lest she should wake; but though he knew that if she awoke she would not let him go, he could not leave her without saying good-bye. And so coming near he stooped over her and very gently kissed her soft cheek and sweet mouth and murmured, "Good-bye, sweet mother." Then, very cautiously, like a shy, little wild animal he stole out of the cavern. Once outside, in the early morning light, he started running as fast as he could, jumping from stone to stone in the rough places, and scrambling through the dew-laden bushes and creepers, until, hot and panting, he arrived down at the very foot of the hill.

Then it was easier walking, and he went on a little until he heard a voice crying, "Martin! Martin!" and, looking back, he saw the Lady of the Hills standing on a great stone near the foot of the mountain, gazing sadly after him. "Martin, oh, my child, come back to me," she called, stretching out her arms towards him. "Oh, Martin, I cannot leave the hills to follow you and shield you from harm and save you from death. Where will you go? Oh me, what shall I do without you?"

For a little while he stood still, listening with tears in his eyes to her words, and wavering in his mind; but very soon he thought of the great blue water once more and could not go back, but began to run again, and went on and on for a long distance before stopping to rest. Then he looked back, but he could no longer see her form standing there on the stone.

All that day he journeyed on towards the ocean over a great plain. There were no trees and no rocks nor hills, only grass on the level earth, in some places so tall that the spikes, looking like great white ostrich plumes, waved high above his head. But it was easy walking, as the grass grew in tussocks or bunches, and underneath the ground was bare and smooth so that he could walk easily between the bunches.

He wondered that he did not get to the sea, but it was still far off, and so the long summer day wore to an end, and he was so tired that he could scarcely lift his legs to walk. Then as he went slowly on in the fading light, where the grass was short and the evening primroses were opening and filling the desert air with their sweet perfume, he all at once saw a little grey old man not above six inches in height standing on the ground right before him, and staring fixedly at him with great, round, yellow eyes.

"You bad boy!" exclaimed this curious little old man; whereupon Martin stopped in his walk and stood still, gazing in the greatest surprise at him.

"You bad boy!" repeated the strange little man.

The more Martin stared at him the harder he stared back at Martin, always with the same unbending severity in his small, round, grey face. He began to feel a little afraid, and was almost inclined to run away; then he thought it would be funny to run from such a very small man as this, so he stared bravely back once more and cried out, "Go away!"

"You bad boy!" answered the little grey man without moving.

"Perhaps he's deaf, just like that other old man," said Martin to himself, and throwing out his arms he shouted at the top of his voice, "Go away!"

And away with a scream he went, for it was only a little grey burrowing owl after all! Martin laughed a little at his own foolishness in mistaking that common bird he was accustomed to see every day for a little old man.

By-and-by, feeling very tired, he sat down to rest, and just where he sat grew a plant with long white flowers like tall thin goblets in shape. Sitting on the grass he could see right into one of the flower-tubes, and presently he noticed a little, old, grey, shrivelled woman in it, very, very small, for she was not longer than the nail of his little finger. She wore a grey shawl that dragged behind her, and kept getting under her feet and tripping her up. She was most active, whisking about this way and that inside the flower; and at intervals she turned to stare at Martin, who kept getting nearer and nearer to watch her until his face nearly touched the flower; and whenever she looked at him she wore an exceedingly severe expression on her small dried-up countenance. It seemed to Martin that she was very angry with him for some reason. Then she would turn her back on him, and tumble about in the tube of the flower, and gathering up the ends of her shawl in her arms, begin dusting with great energy; then hurrying out once more she would shake the dust from her big funny shawl in his eyes. At last he carefully raised a hand and was just going to take hold of the queer, little old dame with his forefinger and thumb when up she flew. It was only a small grey twilight moth!

Very much puzzled and confused, and perhaps a little frightened at these curious deceptions, he laid himself down on the grass and shut his eyes so as to go to sleep; but no sooner had he shut his eyes than he heard a soft, soft little voice calling, "Martin! Martin!"

He started up and listened. It was only a field cricket singing in the grass. But often as he lay down and closed his eyes the small voice called again, plainly as possible, and oh, so sadly, "Martin! Martin!"

It made him remember his beautiful mother, now perhaps crying alone in the cave on the mountain, no little Martin resting on her bosom, and he cried to think of it. And still the small voice went on calling, "Martin! Martin!" sadder than ever, until, unable to endure it longer, he jumped up and ran away a good distance, and at last, too tired to go any further, he crept into a tussock of tall grass and went to sleep.

CHAPTER XVII

THE OLD MAN OF THE SEA

NEXT day Martin journeyed on in the old way, jumping up and taking a good long run, then dropping into a trot, then a walk, and finally sitting down to rest. Then up again and another run, and so on. But although feeling hungry and thirsty, he was so full of the thought of the great blue water he was going to see, so eager to look upon it at last after wishing for it so long, that he hardly gave himself any time to hunt for food. Nor did he think of his mother of the hills, alone to-day, and grieving at his loss, so excited was he at the prospect of what lay before him.

A little past noon he began to hear a low murmuring sound that seemed in the earth beneath him, and all about him, and in the air above him; but he did not know that it was the sound of the sea. At length he came to a place where the earth rose up in long ridges of yellow sand, on which nothing grew but scattered tufts of stiff yellow grass. As he toiled over the loose sand, sometimes sinking ankle-deep in it, the curious deep murmuring sound he had heard for so long grew louder and louder, until it was like the sound of a mighty wind in a wood, but deeper and hoarser, rising and falling, and at intervals broken by great throbs, as of thunder echoed and re-echoed among the distant hills. At length he had toiled over the last ridge of sand; and then all at once the world —his world of solid earth at all events—came to an abrupt end; for no more ground on which to set a foot was before him, but only the ocean — that ocean which he had wanted so badly, and had loved at a distance more than the plains and hills, and all they contained to delight him! How wide, how vast it was, stretching away to where it melted into the low sky, its immense grey-blue surface broken into ten thousand thousand waves, lit with white crests that came in sight and vanished like lightning flashes! How tremendous, how terrible it was in its agitation — O the world had nothing to compare with it, nothing to hold his heart after it; and it was well that the earth was silent, that it only gazed upon it with the sun and moon and stars, listening day and night for ever to the great voice of the sea!

Only by lying flat on his chest could Martin look down over the edge of the awful cliff, which is one of the highest in the world; and then the sight of the sea swirling and beating at the foot of that stupendous black precipice, sending up great clouds of spray in its fury, made him shudder, it was so awful to look upon. But he could not stir from that spot; there he stayed lying flat on his chest, gazing and gazing, feeling neither hunger nor thirst, forgetful of the beautiful woman he had called mother, and of everything besides. And as he gazed, little by little, that great tumult of the waves grew less; they no longer lifted themselves up, wave following wave, to beat upon the cliff, and make it tremble; but sank lower and lower; and at last drew off from the precipice, leaving at its foot a long narrow strip of sand and shingle exposed to sight. A solemn calm fell upon the waste of waters; only near the shore it continued to move a little, rising and falling like the chest of a sleeping giant, while along the margin small waves continued to form and break in white foam on the shingle with a perpetual low moaning sound. Further out it was quite calm, its surface everywhere flushed with changing violet, green, and rosy tints: in a little while these lovely colours faded as from a sunset cloud, and it was all deep dark blue: for the sun had gone, and the shadows of evening were over land and sea. Then Martin, his little heart filled with a great awe and a great joy, crept away a few yards from the edge of the cliff and coiled himself up to sleep in a hollow in the soft warm sand.

On the following morning, after satisfying his hunger and thirst with some roots which he had not to go very far to find, he returned to watch the sea once more, and there he remained, never removing his eyes from the wonderful scene until the sun was directly over his head; then, when the sea was calm once more, he got up and started to walk along the cliff.

Keeping close to the edge, occasionally stopping to lie down on his chest and peer over, he went on and on for hours, until the afternoon tide once more covered the strip of shingled beach, and the waves rising high began to beat with a sound like thunder against the tremendous cliff, making the earth tremble under him. At length he came to a spot where there was a great gap in the line of the cliff, where in past times a portion of it had tumbled down, and the stupendous masses of rock had rolled far out into the sea, and now formed islands of black jagged rock, standing high above the water. Here among the rocks boiled the sea and roared its loudest, churning its waters into masses of white froth. Here a fresh wonder met his sight: a number of big animals un-like any creature he had ever seen before were lying prone on the rocks just out of the reach of the waves that beat round them. At first they looked like cows, then he saw that they had neither horns nor legs, that their heads were like dogs' but without ears, and that they had two great flapper-shaped feet on their chests with which they walked or crawled upon the rocks whenever a wave broke on them, causing them to move a little higher.

They were sea-lions, a very big sort of seal, but Martin had never heard of such a creature, and being anxious to look more closely at them he went into the gap, and began cautiously climbing down over the broken masses of rock and clay until he got quite near the sea. Lying there on a flat rock he became absorbed in watching these strange dog-headed legless cattle of the sea; for he now had them near, and they could see him, and occasionally one would lift its head and gaze earnestly at him out of large dark eyes that were soft and beautiful like the eyes of the doe that came to him on the hills. O how

I

glad he was to know that the sea, the mighty waters
roaring so loud as if in wrath, had its big beasts too
for him to love, like the hills and plains with their
cattle and deer and horses!

But the tide was still rising, and very soon the
biggest waves began to come quite over the rocks,
rolling the big beasts over and even washing them
off, and it angered them when the waves struck them,
and they roared aloud, and by-and-by they began
to go away, some disappearing beneath the water,
others with heads above the surface swimming away
out into the open sea, until all were gone. Martin
was sorry to lose them, but the sight of the sea
tumbling and foaming on the rocks still held him
there, until all the rocks but one had been covered
by the waters, and this one was a great black jagged
rock close to the shore, not above twenty or thirty
yards from him. Against this mass of rock the waves
continued to dash themselves with a mighty noise,
sending up a cloud of white foam and spray at every
blow. The sight and sound fascinated him. The sea
appeared to be talking, whispering, murmuring,
and crying out aloud to him in such a manner that
he actually began trying to make out what it was
saying. Then up would come a great green wave
rushing and moaning, to dash itself to pieces right
before his face; and each time it broke against the
rock and rose high up, it took a fantastic shape that
began to look more and more the shape of a man.
Yes, it was unmistakably like a monstrous grey old
man, with a vast, snow-white beard, and a world

of disordered white hair floating over and round its head. At all events it was white for a moment, then it looked green—a great green beard which the old man took with his two hands and twisted just as a washerwoman twists a blanket or counterpane, so as to wring the water out of it.

Martin stared at this strange uncouth visitor from the sea; while he in turn, leaning over the rock, stared back into Martin's face with his immense fishy eyes. Every time a fresh wave broke over him, lifting up his hair and garments, which were of brown seaweed and all rags and tatters, it seemed to annoy him somewhat; but he never stirred; and when the wave retired he would wring the water out once more and blow a cloud of sea-spray from his beard. At length, holding out his mighty arms towards Martin, he opened his great, cod-fish mouth, and burst into a hoarse laugh, which sounded like the deep laughter-like cries of the big black-backed gulls. Still, Martin did not feel at all afraid of him, for he looked good-natured and friendly.

"Who are you?" shouted Martin at last.

"Who be I?" returned the man-shaped monster in a hoarse, sea-like voice. "Ho, ho, ho—now I calls that a good un! Why, little Martin, that I've knowed all along, I be Bill. Leastways, that's what they called me afore: but I got promotion, and in consekence I'm called the Old Man of the Sea."

"And how did you know I was Martin?"

"How did I know as you was Martin? Why, bless your innocent heart, I knowed it all along of course. How d'ye think I wouldn't know that? Why, I no sooner saw you there among them rocks than I says to myself, 'Hullo,' says I, 'bless my eyes if that ain't Martin looking at my cows,' as I calls 'em. Of course I knowed as you was Martin."

"And what made you go and live in the sea, Old —Bill?" questioned Martin, "and why did you grow so big?"

"Ho, ho, ho!" laughed the giant, blowing a great cloud of spray from his lips. "I don't mind telling you that. You see, Martin, I ain't pressed for time. Them blessed bells is nothing to me now, not being in the foc'sle trying to git a bit of a snooze. Well, to begin, I were born longer ago than I can tell in a old town by the sea, and my father he were a sailor-man, and was drowned when I were very small; then my mother she died just becoz every man that belonged to her was drowned. For those as lives by the sea, Martin, mostly dies in the sea. Being a orphan I were brought up by Granny. I were very small then, and used to go and play all day in the marshes, and I loved the cows and water-rats and all the little beasties, same as you, Martin. When I were a bit growed Granny says to me one day, 'Bill, you go to sea and be a sailor-boy,' she says, 'becoz I've had a dream,' she says, 'and it's wrote that you'll never git drowned.' For you see, Martin, my Granny were a wise woman. So to the sea I goes, and, boy and man, I was on a many voyages to Turkey and Injy and the Cape and the West Coast and Ameriky, and all round the world forty times over. Many and many's the time I was shipwrecked and overboard, but I never got drowned. At last, when I were gitting a old man, and not much use by reason of the rheumatiz and stiffness in the jints, there was a mutiny in our ship when we was off the Cape; and the captin and mate they was killed. Then comes my turn, becoz I went agin the men, d'ye see, and they wasn't a-going for to pardon me that. So out they had me on deck and began to talk about how they'd finish me—rope, knife, or bullet. 'Mates,' says I, 'shoot me if you like and I'll die comforbly; or run a knife into me, which is better still; or string me up to the yard-arm, which is the most comforble thing I know. But don't you go and put me into the sea,' says I, ' becoz it's wrote that I ain't never going to git drowned, and you'll have all your trouble for nothing,' says I. That made 'em larf a most tremenjous larf. 'Old Bill,' says they, 'will have his little joke.' Then they brings up some iron stowed in the hold, and with ropes and chains they ties well-nigh half a ton of it to my legs and arms, then lowers me over the side. Down I went, in course, which made 'em larf louder than afore; and I were fathoms and fathoms under water afore I stopped hearing them larf. At last I comes down to the bottom of the sea, and glad I were to git there, becoz now I couldn't go no further. There I lies doubled up like a old sea-sarpint along of the rocks, but warm and comforble like. Last of all, the ropes and chains they got busted off becoz of my growing so big and strong down there, and up I comes to blow like a grampus, for I were full of water by reason that it had soaked into me. So that's how I got to be the Old Man of the Sea, hundreds and hundreds of years ago."

"And do you like to be always in the sea, Old Bill?" asked Martin.

"Ho, ho, ho!" laughed the monster. "That's a good 'un, little Martin! Do I like it? Well, it's better than being a sailor-man in a ship, I can tell 'ee. That were a hard life, with nothing good except perhaps the baccy. I were very fond of baccy once before the sea put out my pipe. Likewise of rum. Many's the time I've been picked up on shore that drunk, Martin, you wouldn't believe it, I were that fond of rum. Sometimes, down here, when I remember how good it tasted, I open my mouth wide and takes down a big gulp of sea water, enough to fill a hogshead; then I comes up and blows it all out again just like a old grampus."

And having said this, he opened his vast cavernous mouth and roared out his hoarse ho, ho, ho! louder than before, and at the same time he rose up higher above the water and the black rock he had been leaning on, until he stood like a stupendous tower above Martin — a man-shaped tower of water and spray, and white froth and brown seaweed. Then he slowly fell backwards out upon the sea, and falling upon the sea caused so mighty a wave that it went high over the black rock and washed the face of the cliff, sweeping Martin back among the rocks.

When the great wave retired, and Martin, half-choked with water and half-dazed, struggled on to his feet, he saw that it was night, and a cloudy, black sky was above, and the black sea beneath him. He had not seen the light fade, and had perhaps fallen asleep and seen and talked with that old sea monster in a dream. But now he could not escape from his position down in the gap, just above the roaring waves. There he had to stay, sheltered in a cavity in the rock, and lying there, half sleeping and half waking, he had that great voice of the sea in his ears all night.

CHAPTER XVIII

AFTER a night spent in the roar of the sea, a drenched and bruised prisoner among the rocks, it was nice to see the dawn again. No sooner was it light than Martin set about trying to make his escape. He had been washed by that big wave into a deep cleft among the rocks and masses of hard clay, and shut in there he could not see the water nor anything excepting a patch of sky above him. Now he began climbing over the stones and crawling and forcing himself through crevices and other small openings, making little progress, for he was sore from his bruises and very weak from his long fast, and at intervals, tired and beaten, he would drop down crying with pain and misery. But Martin was by nature a very resolute little boy, and after two or three minutes' rest his tears would cease, and he would be up struggling on determinedly as before.

He was like some little wild animal when it finds itself captive in a cage or box or room, who tries without ceasing to find a way out. There may be no way, but it will not give up trying to find one. And at last, after so much trying, Martin's efforts were rewarded: he succeeded in getting into the steep passage by which he had come down to the sea on the previous day, and in the end got to the top of the cliff once more. It was a great relief, and after resting a little while he began to feel glad and happy at the sight before him: there was the glorious sea again, not as he had seen it before, its wide surface roughened by the wind and flecked with foam; for now the water was smooth, but not still; it rose and fell in vast rollers, or long waves that were like ridges, wave following wave in a very grand and ordered manner. And as he gazed, the clouds broke and floated away, and the sky grew clear and bright, and then all at once the great red sun came up out of the waters!

But it was impossible for him to stay there longer when there was nothing to eat; his extreme hunger compelled him to get up and leave the cliff and the sandy hills behind it; and then for an hour or two he walked feebly about searching for sweet roots, but finding none. It would have gone hard with him then if he had not seen some low, dark-looking bushes at a distance on the dry, yellow plain, and gone to them. They looked like yew-bushes, and when he got to them he found that they were thickly covered with small berries; on some bushes they were purple-black, on others crimson, but all were ripe, and many small birds were there feasting on them. The berries were pleasant to the taste, and he feasted with the little birds on them until his hunger was satisfied; and then, with his mouth and fingers stained purple with the juice, he went to sleep in the shade of one of the bushes. There, too, he spent the whole of that day and the night, hearing the low murmur of the sea when waking, and when morning came he was strong and happy once more, and, after filling himself with the fruit, set off to the sea again.

Arrived at the cliff, he began walking along the edge, and in about an hour's time came to the end of it, for there it sloped down to the water, and before him, far as he could see, there was a wide, shingled beach with low sand-hills behind it. With a shout of joy he ran down to the margin, and the rest of that day he spent dabbling in the water, gathering beautiful shells and seaweed and strangely painted pebbles into heaps, then going on and on again, still picking up more beautiful riff-raff on the margin, only to leave it all behind him at last. Never had he spent a happier day, and when it came to an end he found a sheltered spot not far from the sea, so that when he woke in the night he would still hear the deep, low murmur of the waves on the beach.

Many happy days he spent in the same way, with no living thing to keep him company, except the little white and grey sanderlings that piped so shrill and clear as they flitted along the margin before him; and the great sea-gulls that uttered hoarse, laughter-like cries as they soared and hovered above his head. "Oh, happy birds!" exclaimed Martin, clapping his hands, and shouting in answer to their cries.

Every day Martin grew more familiar with the sea, and loved it more, and it was his companion

and playmate. He was bolder than the little restless
sanderlings that ran and flitted before the advancing
waves, and so never got their pretty white and grey
plumage wet: often he would turn to meet the coming
wave, and let it break round and rush past him, and
then in a moment he would be standing knee-deep
in the midst of a great sheet of dazzling white foam,
until with a long hiss as it fled back, drawing the round
pebbles with it, it would be gone, and he would laugh
and shout with glee. What a grand old play-fellow
the sea was! And it loved him, like the big spotted
cat of the hills, and only pretended to be angry with
him when it wanted to play, and would do him no
harm. And still he was not satisfied, but grew bolder
and bolder, putting himself in its power and trusting
to its mercy. He could play better with his clothes
off; and one day, chasing a great receding wave as far
as it would go, he stood up bravely to encounter
the succeeding wave, but it was greater than the
last, and lifting him in its great green arms it carried
him high up till it broke with a mighty roar on the
beach; then instead of leaving him stranded there
it rushed back still bearing him in its arms out into
the deep. Further and further from the shore it
carried him, until he became terrified, and throwing
out his little arms towards the land, he cried aloud,
"Mother! Mother!"

He was not calling to his own mother far away
on the great plain; he had forgotten her. Now he
only thought of the beautiful Woman of the Hills,
who was so strong, and loved him and made him

call her "Mother"; and to her he cried in his need for help. Now he remembered her warm, protecting bosom, and how she had cried every night at the fear of losing him; how when he ran from her she followed him, calling to him to return. Ah, how cold was the sea's bosom, how bitter its lips!

Struggling still with the great wave, struggling in vain, blinded and half-choked with salt water, he was driven violently against a great black object tumbling about in the surf, and with all the strength of his little hands he clung to it. The water rolled over him, and beat against him, but he would not lose his hold; and at last there came a bigger wave and lifted him up and cast him right on to the object he was clinging to. It was as if some enormous monster of the sea had caught him up and put him in that place, just as the Lady of the Hills had often snatched him up from the edge of some perilous precipice to set him down in a safe place.

There he lay exhausted, stretched out at full length, so tossed about on the billows that he had a sensation of being in a swing; but the sea grew quiet at last, and when he looked up it was dark, the stars glittering in the dim blue vault above, and the smooth, black water reflecting them all round him, so that he seemed to be floating suspended between two vast, starry skies, one immeasurably far above, the other below him. All night, with only the twinkling, trembling stars for company, he lay there, naked, wet, and cold, thirsty with the bitter taste of sea-salt in his mouth, never daring to stir, listening to the continual lapping sound of the water.

Morning dawned at last; the sea was green once more, the sky blue, and beautiful with the young, fresh light. He was lying on an old raft of black, water-logged spars and planks lashed together with chains and rotting ropes. But alas! there was no shore in sight, for all night long he had been drifting, drifting further and further away from land.

A strange habitation for Martin, the child of the plain, was that old raft! It had been made by ship-wrecked mariners, long, long ago, and had floated about the sea until it had become of the sea, like a half-submerged floating island; brown and many-coloured seaweeds had attached themselves to it; strange creatures, half plant and half animal, grew on it; and little shell-fish and numberless slimy, creeping things of the sea made it their dwelling-place. It was about as big as the floor of a large room, all rough, black, and slippery, with the seaweed floating like ragged hair many yards long around it, and right in the middle of the raft there was a large hole where the wood had rotted away. Now, it was very curious that when Martin looked over the side of the raft he could see down into the clear, green water a few fathoms only; but when he crept to the edge of the hole and looked into the water there, he was able to see ten times further down. Looking in this hole, he saw far down a strange, fish-shaped creature, striped like a zebra, with long spines on its back, moving about to and fro. It disappeared, and then, very much further down, something moved, first like a shadow, then like a great, dark form; and as it came up higher it took the shape of a man, but dim and vast like a man-shaped cloud or shadow that floated in the green translucent water. The shoulders and head appeared; then it changed its position and the face was towards him with the vast eyes, that had a dim, greyish light in them, gazing up into his. Martin trembled as he gazed, not exactly with fear, but with excitement, because he recognised in this huge water-monster under him that Old Man of the Sea who had appeared and talked to him in his dream when he fell asleep among the rocks. Could it be, although he was asleep at the time, that the Old Man really had appeared before him, and that his eyes had been open just enough to see him?

By-and-by the cloud-like face disappeared, and did not return though he watched for it a long time. Then sitting on the black, rotten wood and brown seaweed he gazed over the ocean, a vast green, sunlit expanse with no shore and no living thing upon it. But after a while he began to think that there was some living thing in it, which was always near him though he could not see what it was. From time to time the surface of the sea was broken just as if some huge fish had risen to the surface and then sunk again without showing itself. It was something very big, judging from the commotion it made in the water; and at last he did see it or a part of it—a vast brown object which looked like a gigantic man's shoulder, but it might have been the back of a whale. It was no sooner seen than gone, but in a very short time after its appearance cries as of birds were heard at a great distance. The cries came from various directions, growing louder and louder, and before long Martin saw many birds flying towards him.

On arrival they began to soar and circle round above him, all screaming excitedly. They were white birds with long wings and long sharp beaks, and were very much like gulls, except that they had an easier and swifter flight.

Martin rejoiced to see them, for he had been in the greatest terror at the strangeness and loneliness of the sea now that there was no land in sight. Sitting on the black raft he was constantly thinking of the warning words his mother of the hills had spoken— that the sea would kiss him with cold salt lips and take him down into the depths where he would never see the light again. O how strange the sea was to him now, how lonely, how terrible! But birds that with their wings could range over the whole world were of the land, and now seemed to bring the land near him with their white forms and wild cries. How could they help him? He did not know, he did not ask; but he was not alone now that they had come to him, and his terror was less.

And still more birds kept coming; and as the morning wore on the crowd of birds increased until they were in hundreds, then in thousands, perpetually wheeling and swooping and rising and hovering over

him in a great white cloud. And they were of many
kinds, mostly white, some grey, others sooty brown
or mottled, and some wholly black. Then in the midst
of the crowd of birds he saw one of great size wheeling
about like a king or giant among the others, with
wings of amazing length, wild eyes of a glittering
yellow, and a yellow beak half as long as Martin's
arm, with a huge vulture-like hook at the end. Now
when this mighty bird swooped close down over his
head, fanning him with its immense wings, Martin
again began to be alarmed at its formidable appearance; and as more and more birds came, with more
of the big kind, and the wild outcry they made
increased, his fear and astonishment grew; then all
at once these feelings rose to extreme terror and
amazement at the sight of a new bird-like creature
a thousand times bigger than the largest one in the
circling crowd above, coming swiftly towards him.
He saw that it was not flying, but swimming or
gliding over the surface of the sea; and its body
was black, and above the body were many immense
white wings of various shapes, which stood up like
a white cloud.

Overcome with terror he fell flat on the raft, hiding
his face in the brown seaweed that covered it; then
in a few minutes the sea became agitated and rocked
him in his raft, and a wave came over him which
almost swept him into the sea. At the same time
the outcry of the birds was redoubled until he was
nearly deafened by their screams, and the screams
seemed to shape themselves into words. "Martin!

Martin!" the birds seemed to be screaming. "Look up, Martin, look up, look up!" The whole air above and about him seemed to be full of the cries, and every cry said to him, "Martin! Martin! look up! look up!"

Although dazed with the awful din and almost fainting with terror and weakness, he could not resist the command. Pressing his hands on the raft he at last struggled up to his knees, and saw that the feared bird-like monster had passed him by: he saw that it was a ship with a black hull, its white sails spread, and that the motion of the water and the wave that swept over him had been created by the ship as it came close to the raft. It was now rapidly gliding from him, but still very near, and he saw a crowd of strange-looking rough men, with sun-browned faces and long hair and shaggy beards, leaning over the bulwarks staring at him. They had seen with astonishment the corpse, as they thought, of a little naked white boy lying on the old black raft, with a multitude of sea-birds gathered to feed on him; now when they saw him get up on his knees and look at them, they uttered a great cry, and began rushing excitedly hither and thither, to pull at ropes and lower a boat. Martin did not know what they were doing; he only knew that they were men in a ship, but he was now too weak and worn-out to look at or think of more than one thing at a time, and what he was looking at now was the birds. For no sooner had he looked up and seen the ship than their wild cries ceased, and they rose up and up like a white cloud to scatter far and wide over sky and sea.

K

For some moments he continued watching them, listening to their changed voices, which now had a very soft and pleasant sound, as if they were satisfied and happy. It made him happy to hear them, and he lifted his hands up and smiled; then, relieved of his terror and overcome with weariness, he closed his eyes and dropped once more full length upon his bed of wet seaweed. At that the men stared into each other's faces, a very strange startled look coming into their eyes. And no wonder! For long, long months, running to years, they had been cruising in those lonely desolate seas, thousands of miles from home, seeing no land nor any green thing, nor dear face of woman or child: and now by some strange chance a child had come to them, and even while they were making all haste to rescue it, putting their arms out to take it from the sea, its life had seemingly been snatched from them!

But he was only sleeping.

POEMS

THE LONDON SPARROW

A HUNDRED years it seemeth since I lost thee,
O beautiful world of birds, O blessèd birds,
That come and go!—the thrush, the golden-bill
That sweetly fluteth after April rain,
In forest depths the cuckoo's mystic voice,
And in the breezy fields the yellowhammer,
And over all the mounting lark, that makes
The blue heaven palpitate with ecstasy!
Nor in this island only: far beyond
The seas encircling it swift memory flies
To other brighter lands, and leaves behind
The swallow and the dove: in hot sweet woods
The gaudy parrot screams; reedy and vast
Stretch ibis- and flamingo-haunted marshes.

I from such worlds removed to this sad world
Of London we inhabit now together,
O Sparrow, often in my loneliness,
No other friend remaining, turn to thee,
Like some imprisoned wretch, who in his cell
A cricket hears, and listening to its chirp,
Forgets the vanished sunshine and the laughter.
Not oft, O wingèd Arab of the streets,
Thou dusty little scavenger—a bird

149

Ambitious bard should blush to name—not oft
Canst claim such victory: for I have known
The kings and glorious nobles of the race
Whose homely mean ambassador thou art;—
Imperial-crested birds in purple clothed
And splendid scarlet, swans in bridal white,
And many a rainbow-tinted tanager.

Ah! how couldst thou thy birthright, liberty
In breezy woodlands, where were springs for thirst
And many-flavoured fruits to feed upon,
Resign for such a place?—to live long years
From nature sweet in exile voluntary,
Nourished on mouldy crumbs, ignoble bird!
Imprisoned in a lurid atmosphere
That maketh all things black and desolate,
Until, as in a coin illegible
To keenest Antiquary, lost are all
The signs that mark thy kind—the pretty gloss
That Nature gave thee clouded and confounded,
Till to the ornithologist thou art
A bird ambiguous: to others, too,
A thing offensive. Sometimes even I,
Aroused to fury by thy barrel-organ
That puts my thoughts to flight, would gladly hale
    thee
Before the magistrate. For thou hast not
The coyness of thy kind—for awful might
No veneration; noisy, impudent,
Begrimed with soot, the chimney-sweep of birds
To minds æsthetic.

Roughly have I used
The liberty of a friend, and yet I know
I love thee, Sparrow, and thy voice to me—
A dweller once in summer-lands—brings back
Responsive joy, as unto him that walks,
Pensive at eventide, the robin's song
'Midst wintry loneliness. Oh, my lost Muse,
If aught of thy sweet spirit is remaining
After my long neglect, in gratitude
To this my frequent, welcome visitor,
Whose little pipe from out discordant noises
Springs like a flower amidst a waste of rocks
To cheer my exile, I will strike again
The quaint and rust-corroded instrument
I played of yore, and to the Sparrow sing
My latest song, albeit now the chords
Give 'neath my touch an unfamiliar sound
To sadden me—the note of time and change.

At dawn thy voice is loud—a merry voice
When other s   ɩs are few and faint. Before
The muffled thunders of the Underground
Begin to shake the houses, and the noise
Of eastward t   fills the thoroughfares,
Thy voice then welcomes day. Oh what a day!—
How foul and haggard-faced! See, where she comes
In garments ⸢   ⸣l discoloured mists
Stealing unt   st with noiseless foot
Through dim   ken streets. Is she not like,
As sister is to sister, unto her
Whose stainèd cheeks the nightly rains have wet

And made them grey and seamed and desolate,
Beneath the arches of the bitter bridge?
And thou, O Sparrow, from the windy ledge
Where thou dost nestle—creaking chimney-pots
For softly-sighing branches; sooty slates
For leafy canopy; rank steam of slums
For flowery fragrance, and for starlit woods
This waste that frights, a desert desolate
Of fabrics gaunt and grim and smoke-begrimed,
By goblin misery haunted, scowling towers
Of cloud and stone, gigantic tenements
And castles of despair, by spectral gleams
Of fitful lamps illumined,—from such place
Canst thou, O Sparrow, welcome day so foul?
Ay, not more blithe of heart in forests dim
The golden-throated thrush awakes, what time
The leaves a-tremble whisper to the breath,
The flowery breath, of morning azure-eyed!
Never a morning comes but I do bless thee,
Thou brave and faithful Sparrow, living link
That binds us to the immemorial past,
O blithe heart in a house so melancholy,
And keeper for a thousand gloomy years
Of many a gay tradition, heritor
Of Nature's ancient cheerfulness, for thee
'Tis ever Merry England! Never yet,
In thy companionship of centuries
With man in lurid London, didst regret
Thy valiant choice,—yea, even from the time
When all its low-roofed rooms were sweet with scents
From summer fields, where shouting children plucked

The floating lily from the reedy Fleet,
Scaring away the timid water-hen.

Awake at morn when still the wizard Sleep
Refracts from twilight mists the broken rays
Of consciousness, I hear thy lulling voice,
Like water softly warbling, or like wind
That wanders in the ancient moonlit trees.
And lo, with breezy feet I roam abroad;
Before me startled from the shadowy fern
Upsprings the antlered deer and flees away,
And moors before me open measureless
Whereon I seek for Morning washed in dews
Immaculate. To other realms I fly
To wait its coming, walking where the palms
Unmoving stand like pillars that uphold
Some hoary vast cathedral. Lift my heart
To thee, O holy daughter of the sun—
Sweet harbinger—the Dawn! The stars grow pale,
And I am fainting by the way, oppressed
With incense from a thousand forest flowers
All prescient of thy coming! Lo, how vast,
From mist and cloud the awful mountains rise,
Where ever up with incorporeal feet
I climb to meet the dead Peruvian's god!
O swift approaching glory, blind me not
With shafts ineffable! But re-awake
In me the sacred passion of the past,
Long quenched in blood by spirits uninformed
That slew thy worshippers! My senses swim,—
Sustain, or bear me back to earth! My feet

Scarce feel the rolling cloud, or touch they still
The awful summit of the world? Far, far
Beneath, the dark blue ocean moves, the waves
Lift up their lightning crests; the lonely earth
Is jubilant; the rivers laugh; the hills
In forests clothed, or soaring crowned with snow
In barren everlasting majesty,
Are all in gold and purple swathed for joy
That thou art coming!

                Vanished is my dream;
Even while I bowed and veiled my eyes before
The insufferable splendour of the sun
It vanished quite, and left me with this pale,
This phantom morning! With my dream thou fled'st,
O blithe remembrancer, and in thy flight
Callest thy prattling fellows, prompters too
Of dreams perchance, from many a cloudy roof
To flit, a noisy rain of sparrows, down
To snatch a hasty breakfast from the roads,
Undaunted by the thund'rous noise and motion:
But like the petrel—fearless, fitful seeker,
The fluctuating bird with ocean's wastes
And rage familiar, tossed with tossing billows—
So, gleaner unregarded, flittest thou—
Now, as of old, and in the years to come,
Nature's one witness, till the murmuring sound
Of human feet unnumbered, like the rain
Of summer pattering on the forest leaves,
Fainter and fainter falling 'midst the ruin,
In everlasting silence dies away.

IN THE WILDERNESS

THOU white-winged gull that far I see
So buoyant in blue heaven soar,
Ah, would thy wings were mine!
How swiftly would I fly this shore
To scenes for which I pine;
Where dwells unsullied loveliness,
With calm and peace divine,
Far in the untrodden wilderness.

My soul is sickened with the stress
Of life, nor more responds to cries
Of those who lose or win
The things they struggle for. The prize,
The battle's dust and din,
Alike I loathe and seek the rest
That dwells the desert in,
Aloof from man on Nature's breast.

There earth with brighter sun is blest—
In purer dew-drops burns its beam,
That gather here, alas!
There many a heron-haunted stream
And many a plain I'd pass,
A thousand, thousand flowers behold
Strew all the wayside grass
With crimson, white, and blue and gold.

There winds would sing to me, the old,
Old sea give forth a solemn sound,
   The wild birds warble mirth;
There would I stop to kiss the ground
   For very love of earth;
And swift away the years would glide,
   Like rills that have their birth
High on the soaring mountain side.

To gaze upon the prospect wide,
Oft on some jutting crag I'd lie
   When blooms its summer crown—
Pale heath and pansy's purple eye,
   The wind-flower, and the brown
And green blades of the bearded grass,
   Whose spears wave up and down,
White sparkling when the wind doth pass.

And there I'd muse and sigh, alas,
This transitory state of ours—
   Whose resting is the tomb—
To liken to such things as flowers,
   A little while that bloom
And sweets of paradise exhale
   From aisles of stormy gloom,
From wood and wold and winding vale.

For everywhere the blossoms frail
I love—to me do preachers seem,
   And have for me a speech
With many a mystic mournful theme;

And subtle things they teach—
(Not like harsh lessons writ with pen)—
　　And inner sense oft reach,
That wakes not in the haunts of men.

The hoary hills I'd liken, when
The flowers in all their fissures blow—
　　The rocks so seamed and grey
With all the length of years they know,
　　And yet to pass away,
Not doomed like things that draw the breath
　　Of life and of decay—
Unto a monument of death.

Memorial there the sleeper hath,
Whose dust before the wind like chaff
　　Has long been scattered wide;
There blooms his living epitaph;
　　And still while time shall glide,
Those letters blooming, fading, speak,
　　Thus flourished he, thus died;
Thus bloomed, thus paled in death his cheek.

Sad are such thoughts, yet who would seek
To blot them from his spirit's page
　　Who on his nothingness
Thinks not—how brief his pilgrimage?
　　Oh, rather let him bless
The thoughts that teach the unwilling sight
　　To look with less and less
Of terror on the coming night.

GWENDOLINE

SHOULD'ST thou come to me again
From the sunshine and the rain,
    With thy laughter sweet and free—
Oh, how should I welcome thee?

Like a streamlet dark and cold,
Kindled into fiery gold,
By a sunbeam swift that cleaves
Downward through the curtained leaves—

So this darkened life of mine
Lit with sudden joy would shine;
And to greet thee I should start
With a great cry in my heart;

Back to drop again; the cry
On my trembling lips would die;
Thou would'st pass to be again
In the sunshine and the rain.

TECLA AND THE LITTLE MEN

A LEGEND OF LA PLATA

IT happened ninety years ago,
Hard by the spot where I was born,
The tragedy of little Tecla:
Scarce half a dozen hoary men
Now the maiden's name remember.
The world has changed, these ancients say,
From what it was;—the plume-like grass
That waved so high, the ostrich blue,
The wild horse and the antlered deer
Are now no more.

                  Here where the plain
Looks on the level marsh and out
Upon the waters of the Plata
An old estancia house once stood:
And I have played upon its site
In boyhood long ago, and traced
'Mong flowering weeds its old foundations.
'Twas here lived Lara and his wife
With their grown-up sons and daughters;
Happy and rich in pasture lands
And in their numerous herds and flocks.
Before the house a level plain
Bestrewn with shells spread shining white;
And often when the moon was up

Here came a troop of Little Men,
No taller than a boy of twelve,
Robust of limb and long of hair,
And wearing cloaks and broad sombreros.
From windows and from open doors
Distinctly could all see and hear them,
Sitting upon the ground in groups,
In shrill excited voices talking;
Or running to and fro; or ranged
Like cricketers about a field,
Playing their games the whole night long.
But if one ventured from the house
To walk upon their chosen field,
Straightway would they quit their game
To chase him back with hooting shrill,
Hurling showers of stones and pebbles
That rattled on the doors and roof
Like hail, and frightened those within.
Of all in Lara's house but one,
Light-hearted Tecla, feared them not.
The youngest of the daughters she,
A little maiden of fifteen,
Winsome in her wayward moods;
Her blithesomeness and beauty made
Perpetual sunshine in the house.
O merrily would Tecla laugh
When pebbles rattled on the door
To see her bearded brothers start,
And mother and sisters wax so pale,
And oft in pure capriciousness
Alone she'd venture forth to sit

A stone's throw from the gate, just on
The margin of that moonlit field;
There in the twilight would she linger
And bravely watch them by the hour,
Standing or running to and fro,
Hailing each other at their sport.

But once, one evening, trembling, pale,
Flying like a fawn pursued
By leaping hounds, flew Tecla home;
In at the open door she rushed
And clasped her mother close, and then
Crept silently away, and in
A corner sobbed herself to rest:
She would not tell what frightened her,
But from that evening nevermore
Would Tecla venture out alone,
When sunset left the world in shadow.
A month went by; then it was seen
A change had fallen on her spirits;
She was no more the merry one—
The bird that warbled all day long:
Infrequent fell her silvery laugh;
And silent, pale, with faltering steps,
And downcast eyes, she paced the floors,
Who yesterday from room to room
Danced fairylike her blithesome measures.

"O say what ails you, daughter mine?
Imposthumes hidden, spasms, rheums,
Catarrhs and wasting calentures,

Have yielded to the juices I
Express from herbs medicinal;
Yet this most subtle malady
Still mocks your mother's love and skill."
"I have no sickness, mother, 'tis
But weakness; for I cannot eat,
Since on one day, long weeks ago,
Each morsel all at once appeared,
Even as I raised it, red with dust,
And thus till now it is with me;
And water limpid from the well,
And milk, grow turbid with red dust
When lifted to my thirsting lips,
Until I loathe all aliment."
"'Tis but a sickly fancy, child,
Born of a weak distempered stomach
That can no longer bear strong food.
But you shall have things delicate
And easy to digest; the stream
Shall give its little silvery fish
To tempt; the marsh its painted eggs
Of snipe and dotterel; sweet curds
Made fragrant with the purple juice
Of thistle bloom I'll make for you
Each day, until the yellow root
Of the wild red vinegar-flower,
With powders made from gizzards dried
Of iron-eating ostriches
Bring back a healthy appetite,
And make your nostrils love again
The steam of roasted armadillo."

Vain was her skill: no virtue dwelt
The wasting maiden to restore
In powders or in root. And soon
The failing footsteps ceased their rounds,
And through the long, long summer days
Her white cheek rested on her pillow.
And often when the moonlight shone
Upon her bed, she, lying still,
Would listen to the plover's cry,
And tinkling of the bell-mare's bell,
Come faintly from the dreamy distance;
Then in her wistful eyes would shine
A light that made her mother weep.

Within the wide old kitchen once
The Laras from their evening meal
Were startled by a piercing cry
From Tecla's room; and rushing in
They found her sobbing on the floor,
Trembling, as white as any ghost.
They lifted her—O easy 'twas
To lift her now, for she was light
As pining egret in their arms—
And laid her on her bed. And when
Her terror left her, and the balm
They gave had soothed her throbbing heart,
Clasped in her mother's arms she told
The story of her malady.

"Do you remember, mother mine,
How once with terror palpitating
Into the house I ran? That eve

Long had I sat beyond the gate
Listening to the shrill-voiced talking
And laughter of the Little People,
And half I wished—oh, was it wrong?—
Yet feared to join them in their games.
When suddenly on my neck I felt
A clasping arm, and in my ear
A voice that whispered: 'Tecla sweet,
A valiant little maid art thou!'
O mother, 'twas a Little Man,
And through the grass and herbage tall,
Soft stealing like a cat, he came,
And leaped upon the stone, and sat
By me! I rose and ran away;
Then fast he followed, crying out:
'Run; tell your mother you have found
A lover who will come full soon
For thee; run, run, thy sisters tell
Thou hast a lover rich in gold
And gems to make them pine with envy!'
And he has caused this weakness, mother;
And often when I lie awake
He comes to peer in at the window,
And smiles and whispers pretty things.
This night he came, and at my side,
Wearing a cloak all beautiful
With scarlet bright embroidery,
He sat and boldly played the lover."

"And what said he? The wicked imp!"
"He asked me if that yellow root

That's bitter to the taste, and all
My wise old mother's medicines
Had made me hungry. Then he held
A golden berry to my mouth—
The fruitlet of the Camambú:
O beautiful it looked, and had
No red or grimy dust upon it!
And when I ate and found it sweet,
And asked with hungry tears for more,
He whispered pleasant promises
Of honied fruits: and then he spoke—
O mother mine, what did he mean!—
Of wanderings over all the earth,
Lit by the moon, above the dim
Vast forests; over tumbling waves,
And hills that soar beyond the clouds.
Then eagerly I started up
For joy to fly away with him
Bird-like above the world, to seek
Green realms; and in his arms he clasped
And raised me from my bed. But soon
As from a dream I screaming woke,
And strove so strongly to be free
He dropped me on the floor and fled."
"O daughter dear, how narrowly
Hast 'scaped! But not to you again
Shall come such moments perilous;
For know, O Tecla, and rejoice
That from this moment dates your cure,
Since like a wise physician I
Up to its hidden source have traced

The evil that afflicted you.
In former days the Little Men
Oft played their wicked pranks, but years
Have passed since any proof they gave
Of their maleficence, since sharp
And bitter lessons given them
By Holy Church had taught these imps
To know their place; and now I too
Shall draw against them sacred weapons."

Next morning to the Monastery
Hard by, where dwelt a brotherhood
Of Friars Dominican, was sent
A messenger, the holy men
To summon to the house of Lara—
To arm with ghostly arms and free
Fair Tecla from these persecutions.

At noon, wrapped in a dusty cloud,
Six mounted Friars came riding in
Their steeds at furious gallop. They,
Rough men, spent no ignoble lives
In barren offices; but broke
The steeds they rode, and pastured herds
Of half-wild cattle, wide around
The ostrich and the puma hunted.
Thus boldly came they—Tecla's knights,
Armed with a flask of holy water,
Nor wanting at their leathern girdles
Long knives and pistols with brass barrels.

Forthwith the blest campaign began;
And through the house and round the house
They walked; on windows, walls and doors
Sprinkling the potent drops that keep
All evil things from entering;
And curses in a learned tongue
They hurled against the Little Men.

O gladly beat the heart within
The breast of every Lara there
For Tecla timely saved! She too
The sweet infection caught, and blest
With hope and health reviving laughed
The silvery laugh too long unheard.

And there was nothing more to do
Now but to finish day so good
With feast and merriment. Then lambs
And sucking pigs were straightway slain
To heap the board hospitable;
While screaming over fields and ditches
Turkeys and ducks were chased to make
A rich repast. Then freely round
Travelled the mighty jugs of wine,
Till supper done the Friar Blas
Snatched the guitar: "Away," he cried,
"With chairs and tables! Let us show
The daughters of the house of Lara
That our most holy Monastery
Can give them partners for the dance!"

Loudly the contra-dance he played,
And sang, while standing in two rows
The ready dancers ranged themselves;
Till on her pillow Tecla smiled
To hear the strings twang merrily:
"O hasten, mother mine," she cried,
"To join the dance, and open wide
The doors so that the sounds may reach me."

And while they danced the Friar Blas
Improvised merry boastful words,
And couplets full of laughing jibes:

"Dost know how to sing, Little Man?
Come sing with a Dominican.

"O when I remember our fight
I must laugh for my victory to-night.

"There conquered you bleed and repine;
Here sing I and drink the red wine.

"I'll preach you a sermon in song—
My sermons are merry not long.

"No more to sweet Tecla aspire,
For know that your rival's a Friar.

"Not wise was your wooing, but cruel,
For who can have fire without fuel?

"Did'st lose her by making her thin?
By fattening perchance I shall win.

"For when the pale maiden gets well
I'll carry her off to my cell;

"For the labourer he looks for his hire,
And hot is the heart of the Friar."

A burst of laughter and applause
Followed the strain. Out rung a peal
Of eldritch laughter echoing theirs!
Sitting and standing, dancers clasped
In joyous attitudes, transfixed,
All silent, motionless, amazed,
They listened as it louder grew—
That laughter demoniacal—
Till jugs and glasses jingled loud
Upon the table, as when hoarse
Deep thunder rumbles near, and doors
And windows shudder in their frames,
And all the solid house is shaken
To its foundations. Slowly it died;
But even as it died they heard
A wailing cry:—far off it seemed,
Still ever growing more remote,
Until they thought 'twas but the sound
The stringed guitar, dropped on the floor,
Gave forth, upon their straining ears
Slow dying in long reverberations.

Up sprang the mother suddenly
Giving a mighty cry, and flew
To Tecla's chamber. After her
The others trooped, and found her there
Weeping beside the empty cot,
Wringing her hands and wailing loud,
Calling on Tecla gone for ever.
In at the open window blew
The fresh night wind; and forth they peered
With straining eyes and faces white,
Their hearts with strange surmisings filled.
Only the moon they saw, ghost-like
In heaven walking: 'neath its light
Immeasurable spread the marsh,
And far off shone the sea-like river;
Only the swelling waves they heard,
Low murmuring to their listening ears
Through the deep silence of the night.

THE OLD MAN OF KENSINGTON GARDENS

I

THE earth is strown with withered leaves;
　　The pale October sun
　　Illumines with his waning beams
The trees of Kensington.

The sere leaves rustle 'neath my tread,—
　　Few on the trees remain:
For summer hark, a sweet lament—
　　The fitful robin's strain.

Too long, too long for me has been
　　This dream of fourscore years;
Since now of all who walked with me
　　But one in flesh appears:

And he an old mysterious man,
　　Whose heart beats blithely still
When on grey cheek and hoary hair
　　The wintry wind blows chill.

When float above grey clouds on clouds;
    When leaves are sere and dead;
When others walk with spirits bowed,
    With sad reluctant tread,

He has no care; his unaged heart
    Some pleasant fancy cheers;
He talks like one that's young; he laughs
    As in the vanished years.

II

Since I played here in childish glee
    O'er three score years and ten
Have passed—since first I knew him here,
    Ancient and hoary then.

An old man with a beard so white;
    While blue-eyed and so fair
Walked with him, ever at his side,
    A child of golden hair.

Oft in the shade those two I saw;
    Until, one summer day,
The old man spied me in his walk
    And called me from my play.

"Come here," cried he, "my pretty boy,
  A playmate waits you here;
And much it will my heart rejoice
  To watch your merry cheer.

"To join in merry hide-and-seek
  Too stiff and old I am,
But still my heart can skip and leap
  And frolic like a lamb."

"Is she your little daughter, sir?"
  Said I. The old man smiled,
And said, "Can one so ancient be
  The father of a child?"

"She is your grandchild then," I urged.
  "That cannot be," he said,
And looked upon his little girl,
  And smiled and shook his head.

"Your great-granddaughter then," said I,
  "This child must surely be?"
"Too young, too young for that," he cried,
  Nor more would answer me.

A merry game at hide-and-seek
  Together then we played;
And in and out among the trees
  I chased the little maid.

And much it did that ancient man
  Rejoice our sport to see;
And like a child he clapped his hands,
  And shook his sides with glee.

And afterwards for full three years,
  On many a summer day,
I met and played with her, till we
  Had grown too old to play.

III

A youth with down upon his cheek
  I bade those two farewell,
And went abroad for seven years
  Beside the Rhine to dwell.

But when that studious time was gone,
  I sought my native shore,
And in the stately Gardens walked
  Of Kensington once more.

And there that ancient man I met,
  Still cheerful as of old,
And by the hand a child he held
  With hair that was like gold.

"Who is this pretty babe?" said I,
    "With pretty eyes so blue?"
"She is the child of that fair child
    That once played here with you.

"A babe in sooth, and not for me
    'Tis now to run about,
And in and out among the trees
    To run from her with shout.

"But by-and-by, when she has grown
    More firm and free of limb,
Some little boy my maid shall know,
    And she shall play with him.

"And I shall laugh to watch their sport;
    For though so old I am,
My heart goes skipping to and fro
    And leaping like a lamb."

I heard, yet scarcely did attend;
    My thoughts were far away—
What cared I how an old man spent
    The remnant of his day?

The fire of youth was in my heart,
    Ambition fired my mind:
I crossed the seas and England left
    A thousand leagues behind.

In courts of kings, in many a camp
 On India's sultry soil,
Full twenty stirring years I spent
 In peace and war's red toil.

Then struck at last in battle down,
 For many a night and day—
Within my breast a bleeding wound—
 A groaning wretch I lay.

And night and day I pined to gaze
 On England's shores again,
Until that journey long was made
 With peril and great pain.

IV

Upon my soil beloved at last,
 When shone the summer sun,
Once more I in the Gardens walked
 Of stately Kensington.

But changed was I, with cheeks so pale
 And hollow with disease!
How slowly I moved towards the shade
 With weak and trembling knees!

While sadly musing there I sat,
    Before my sight appeared
An ancient venerable man,
    With flowing snow-white beard.

'Twas he, that old man I had known
    In boyhood and in youth,
His babe now grown to womanhood—
    The very same in sooth!

Once more we talked beneath the trees,
    As in that long ago;
And gay and garrulous was he;
    I silent, full of woe.

His laugh was frequent, idle words
    Ran ceaseless from his tongue;
Of flowers he babbled, breeze and bird,
    And things that please the young.

I sighed in heaviness of heart,
    And sad was my reply
Of toils and wounds received in wars;
    Of coming home to die.

But still he talked and did not seem
    My words to understand;
And many times to welcome me
    He seized and shook my hand.

M

"O long-lost wanderer, welcome home!"
  He cried. "'Tis sweet to know
Not all are lost for evermore
  That vanished long ago.

"For sometimes, after many years,
  One comes again, a while
To linger here and gladden me
  With a remembered smile.

"But not for long: a restless fire
  Within him ever burns;
His wistful eye at eventide
  Oft to the sunset turns.

"And by-and-by, like passage birds
  That in the night depart,
He goes, nor ever more returns
  To cheer the old man's heart."

V

Each day all through the pleasant June
  I in the Gardens found
That ancient man: his voice subdued
  Grew like a soothing sound

Of babbling waters, or of leaves
    Soft rustling to the wind—
It came on me, my pain appeased,
    To hope restored my mind.

"Though light of foot no more," he cried,
    "But old and stiff I am,
My fancy swallow-like still flies,
    My heart skips like a lamb.

"'Tis sweet to listen from the green
    Old elms, at drowsy noon,
The whisper of the wind-moved leaves,
    The cushat's pleasant croon.

"And when the winter drives me home,
    The fire shall cheerly burn;
And I shall wait beside the glow
    For flowery May's return.

"When evenings lengthen, at my side
    My pretty maid shall sit,
And merrily we'll pass the time
    With tales for winter fit.

"But she, too, shortly from me goes
    To seek another's side;
For now a youth has won her love
    And she shall be his bride.

"And I must pass the time alone;
   But time ere long shall send
A troop of little ones, and soon
   My lonely days shall end.

"I'll choose the prettiest of the lot—
   A little maid—and she,
With eyes like blue forget-me-nots,
   Shall my companion be.

"And when my pretty blue-eyed maid
   Grows firm and free of limb,
A boy of gentle face I'll find
   And she shall play with him."

Thus while he gaily talked and smiled
   New dreams and wishes came:
The maiden dropped her gentle eyes
   And blushed with virgin shame.

"O ever sweetest," I exclaimed,
   "Of all earth's joys is this!
My heart beats at the sacred name
   Of dear domestic bliss!

"No longer will I waste my prime;
   I too shall have a part
In joy at last, and satisfy
   The hunger of my heart.

"Once more I'll cross the ocean wide,
  For here the fight of life
Is passing hard to fight, and I
  Have weary grown of strife.

"But half around the globe, and in
  Another hemisphere,
A better fortune I shall build—
  My peaceful home I'll rear.

"And one shall share that home with me;
  And as in May from earth
Spring fragrant flowerets, children dear
  Shall blossom on my hearth.

"They, too, shall play at hide-and-seek
  Amid the forest trees,
And roam in flowery gardens sweet
  More wild and vast than these.

"And in the autumn of my life
  They oft at day's decline
Shall gather round their hoary sire
  Beneath the spreading vine,

"To listen while he tells the tale
  Of how he long did roam,
In stormy years, in countries strange,
  Before he found a home."

I finished and the old man rose;
  "God speed!" he said, and smiled;
"Come home, my bonny child—no, no,
  You are no more a child!

"For you have grown to womanhood,
  And I perchance did dream
Of one—a little one—that soon
  Like what you were shall seem."

Among the trees they passed from sight;
  I turned to go; before
The sun had set and risen thrice
  I left my native shore.

VI

Now came a time of happiness
  To me in distant lands;
Peace smiled on me and Fortune blessed
  The labour of my hands.

Far in a flowery desert lone,
  In forest green attired—
A virgin paradise—arose
  The home so long desired.

And lord of all the land was I—
  Woods, hills and valleys fair;
And all the flocks and herds were mine
  That grazed in thousands there.

Often by breezy mountains blue,
  And forests without bound,
The flying quarry I pursued
  With horse and horn and hound.

And one with me that home did share,
  My brave and beauteous bride;
And children sweet were born like flowers
  To flourish at our side.

But woe is me! the fatal shade
  That rides the wandering blast,
And follows us in all our ways,
  Found our retreat at last.

I could not dwell upon the grave
  Of all my dear ones lost;
Once more a pilgrim in old age,
  Weary and tempest-tossed,

Sought I through many lands, o'er seas,
  The respite hard to find,
Till time and change in part appeased
  The anguish of my mind.

My wanderings ended where the chase,
　　Life-long, of bliss began:
Here, said I, let me spend the days
　　Left to so old a man.

VII

Once more I in the Gardens walked,
　　Fanned by the summer breeze,
And heard the thrush that all day long
　　Makes music in the trees.

As there I mused a man I met,
　　Wrinkled and old, of slow
And feeble tread, and body bent,
　　And beard as white as snow;

And with him, lending him support,
　　A maiden sweet and grave.
He paused and looked at me, then forth
　　A joyful cry he gave.

"Welcome, O long-lost friend!" cried he.
　　"So many years passed o'er
Since forth you went from us, I dreamed
　　You would return no more.

"It is the way with them; a while
   They take their solace here—
Maiden and youth and merry child—
   Then go I know not where.

"For seldom do these waiting eyes
   See the old face once more:
Far are they scattered—far and wide
   On many a distant shore.

"Shadows and lights and seasons change;
   The birds that to and fro
For ever wander, sing again
   The songs of long ago:

"And all things wander to and fro—
   Sun and bird and breeze—
Only the faces I have known,
   In vain I watch for these.

"My fancy follows them and sees
   Many a loving pair
In flowery groves more green than these,
   Where breathes a balmier air.

"Far off in ocean's thousand isles
   The merry children stray,
And laugh as in the vanished time
   Before they went away.

"But should they—children, man and maid—
　Once more this side the sea
Gather from all their scattered ways,
　More numerous would they be

"Than are the sere autumnal leaves,
　When days grow brief and pale,
And loud roars in the Garden trees
　The rough September gale;

"When all along the Serpentine
　The swallows wildly fly,
Then soar aloft and scatter wide
　Athwart the lowering sky;

"While ever and anon the clouds
　Fling gusts of sudden rain;
And the wind roars; anon dies down,
　Then wakes and roars again:

"And often as it roars and sways
　The groves with giant might,
Fly wild and wide the yellow leaves
　In cloud-like flight on flight.

"Yellow and russet leaves and brown,
　Myriads on myriads still,
In dance tempestuous whirl about
　And all the spaces fill.

"So filled with children, maids and men
　　Would all the Gardens be,
Should they return from all far lands
　　And islands of the sea.

"But they return not: fragrant trees
　　Are theirs and cloudless skies:
The days wear on, they do not heed
　　The ancient memories.

"And still as days and years glide on
　　Old forms to new give place;
Then these depart, and other forms
　　Succeed to go apace.

"O restless hearts, why will they not
　　Rest here in peace with me!
What voices call them o'er the main—
　　In dreams what is't they see!"

Thus as we walked the old man's speech
　　Ran like a babbling stream;
And now I thought it all was real,
　　Now thought it but a dream.

"What can the mystery be?" I cried:
　　"I hear you speak and seem
To be awake, yet all the time
　　I think it is a dream.

"I knew this spot, these elms and oaks,
Unseen for many a year,
Yon open glade and this dim grove—
I played in childhood here.

"But oaks and elms outlive frail man
And flourish ages through;
The vernal green, the leaves they shed,
They year by year renew.

"But nevermore for us the flame
Of youth revives the heart:
For manhood comes, then hoary age,
And soon the old depart.

"Yet you still linger, long ago
Who should have passed from sight;
For here a child I knew you old,
And time has made me white.

"Since last I saw you in this place
Oh, many a changeful year,
Has fled, yet with the selfsame maid
I find you walking here!"

The old man laughed aloud at that.
"It is not so!" cried he;
"The dear companions of my walks
Bide not so long with me.

"She passed from me—this gentle maid
   Will make as fair a bride—
I know not where, but far away
   Our paths have sundered wide.

"And this one has her mother's face—
   The daughter this, my friend—
And she will go the usual way,
   Our rambles soon will end.

"For now a youth with words of love
   Her gentle heart has won,
And she must quit the glades and groves
   Of pleasant Kensington.

"And when the groves are ghostly white,
   When 'neath the sombre cloud
Along the frozen Serpentine
   The merry skaters crowd,

"Beside the hearth I'll sit alone
   Through the long winter hours,
With no one near to share the glow,
   Until the time of flowers.

"But pretty flowers will come full soon;
   And when sweet children rise,
The fairest of them all I'll choose—
   One with her mother's eyes.

"And she shall my companion be
    On many a summer's day,
And I will watch her through the trees
    Glance by in blithesome play."

She turned aside her blushing face:
    The old man smiling sees;
Then from my side they passed away
    Among the Garden trees.

VIII

Now since I sought my land, these last
    Few years of life to spend—
The pale sad years that now perchance
    Are drawing to an end—

Six years have gone o'er me; yet oft
    As in the green retreat
Of stately Kensington I walk,
    That ancient man I meet.

Six years ago she left his side—
    The maid with hair like gold:
And with him totters now a child—
    A little five-year-old.

He talks on cheerful themes; his words
    Flow ceaseless from his tongue—
Of flowers he babbles, breeze and bird,
    And things that please the young.

He strays away: I sit for hours
    And listen to the wind,
And many a whispering dreamy sound
    That lulls my weary mind.

Of marble white and fretted gold,
    Before my fading eye,
The storied strange Memorial soars
    Sparkling against the sky.

Unceasing on my hearing falls,
    By distance made as low
As croon of dove, from all along
    The carriage-crowded Row

The sound of many hoofs and wheels;
    A ceaseless muffled roar,
As of a distant swelling sea
    Breaking along the shore.

It lulls my mind; it dies away;
    Now far it seems, now near:
The trees, the objects round me fade,
    And other scenes appear

And still I hear that sound that is
  A river's rush, while I
Look on old towns—on purple hills,
  On castles floating by.

I talk beneath the linden trees
  To youth and maid I know;
Along the ancient pleasant street
  The people come and go.

They come and gather to a crowd;
  In serried ranks they form,
While ever nearer and more loud
  Is rolled the battle storm.

It dies; the smoke-cloud fades away,
  And pale, with bleeding breast,
O'er weary lands and ocean's waves
  I wander seeking rest.

And when to rest I sit me down
  'Tis 'neath the wild-wood tree;
There stands my steed, there lie my hounds,
  Worn with the chase like me.

Lo, where they come—O darling wife!
  O long-lost children dear!
Ah, wherefore have we wandered wide
  In grief this many a year!

I stretch my arms; alas, it fades—
  That vision sweet—in air!
Then with a sudden cry I wake
  And wildly round me stare.

The ancient man is sitting near:
  "Wake, dreamer, wake!" he cries.
I gaze on him, I strive to pierce
  The meaning of his eyes.

A mystic smile flits o'er his face;
  His touch is on my arm:
"I knew," he says, "that soon again
  This place would cease to charm.

"Again you dream of deserts vast
  Beyond the ocean wide:—
Oh, why have men such restless hearts!
  Why here will they not bide!

"But let them go, since go they will,
  My heart can merry be,
And like the robin blithely sing
  Apart from company."

And thus he ever speaks, and half
  In anger, half in play—
"Dream on," he cries, "of countries far,"
  Then leads his child away.

N

IX

When autumn draweth to a close,
  Oft as the October sun
With transient glory lights the groves
  Of stately Kensington,

Beneath the rustling trees I roam,
  Although the east blows chill,
To taste the passing beams—to know
  That I am living still.

And by my side the old man walks,
  The maid with golden hair—
While I immersed in mournful thoughts
  Heed not their presence there.

The sere leaves flutter on the trees,
  They rustle 'neath my tread:
The sun declines, the slanting beams
  A mystic glory shed.

The leaves that flutter to the earth,
  And far-off fane and spire,
And tower and dome, a moment burn
  With visionary fire.

"O season of black storms and tears,
  Of red and yellow leaf,
And glory of the sun's swift beams,
  Thy troubled period brief

" Full soon must end, and storm and shine
  With thee pass from me here.
The earth, the heavens infinite,
  The pale-faced dying year,

"With all their voices day and night,
  From earth, from ocean loud,
From birds that crying cleave the skies,
  From wind and rain and cloud,

"And from the sun's departing gleams
  Kindling the forests tall,
And thousand thousand withered leaves
  That whirl aloft and fall,

"Are calling, calling me to rise—
  Their voices fill my ear,
They tell me that the mournful time
  Of going forth is near.

"Often have I ere now gone forth,
  Both danger and disease
To brave, and hordes of frantic foes,
  And world-encircling seas;

N 2

"But greater dangers wait me now;
  And, oh, how shall I brave
That blacker sea! oh, there what clouds,
  What shipwreck and what grave

"Perchance, perchance are waiting me!
  Nor on this mournful shore
Is left one friend with farewell speech
  To waft me kindly o'er!"

He laughs to hear—that ancient man—
  A mocking laugh it seems!
"Yes, yes!" he cries, "I understand—
  Still dreaming the old dreams!

"You cannot rest; the dreams of isles
  And regions near the sun,
They will not let you here abide;
  And pale looks Kensington.

"Your friends have gone before, and lone
  And sere the Gardens seem:
Far off in summer-lands you roam—
  You meet them when you dream.

"What wonder? withered are the trees,
  And winds blow coldly here:
But there the spicy woods are green,
  And winterless the year.

"Rich fruits grow there: the birds are gay
   With plumes of splendid dyes:
From flower to flower the children chase
   The blue-winged butterflies.

"There people throng the sunny streets
   In gems and garments white:
Of marble are the palaces,
   And gold and malachite.

"There friends and old companions meet,
   Returned with precious spoil
From many a coast; together feast,
   And rest their hearts from toil.

"And oft from rest the bugle calls,
   To hunt in wood and glen
The tusky boar, or meet in war
   Dark hordes of savage men:

"To chase with fire and thund'rous noise
   The flying Amazon;
And of their treasured gold despoil
   The temples of the sun:

"To pass the azure mountain chains,
   Where vast volcanoes flame,
And riches seek in cities strange,
   And realms without a name.

"Then far to sail the halcyon seas,
    Full many a fragrant isle
To find, where in perpetual peace
    Dwell nations void of guile.

"There often as the wanderer's keel
    Does grate, from grots and bowers
Troop maidens forth, their foreheads wreathed
    With pearls and crimson flowers,

"Singing of peace—eternal peace,
    Within the isle of palms—
Singing a sacred melody
    That care and passion charms.

"O beauteous regions far away
    From this tempestuous shore,—
He dreams of you, and here his place
    Will know him soon no more!

"He dreams of you as others dreamed,
    He can no more delay—
Farewell. O friend of many years,
    God speed you on your way.

"We too, my child and I, shall dream
    When cheerfully does burn
The winter fire—dream eve by eve
    Of flowery May's return.

"And when the flowery May returns,
    And heaven sweetly smiles;
When flit and sing the passage birds
    The songs of other climes—

"The climes for which you sadly sigh—
    Here shall we spend the hours,
And have for friends—my child and I—
    The sunshine and the flowers."

And thus he talks at day's decline,
    With words so wild and vain,
Then homeward leads his little child
    And leaves me to my pain.

X

The days are growing cold and brief,
    And sad the Gardens seem,
As over beds of fallen leaves
    I walk as in a dream.

My blood is thin and I am old;
    Wind, fog, and frost-bound earth
Now drive me shivering in to doze
    All day beside the hearth.

But when the season sweet revives
　With leaf and flower and bee,
When blushing maid at eventide
　Seeks here the trysting tree;

When pipes the thrush at eventide,
　Perchance I shall not hear;
For now I flutter in the wind,
　And I am pale and sere:

I flutter in the wind, for now
　The frosty winds prevail,
And on the tree of life each hour
　My hold is getting frail.

But they will come—you will not fail
　To meet them here—the old,
Old man, and pretty little maid
　With locks of shining gold.

P5